The Art of B

(Spiritual Laws of

The Art of Blissful Living
(Spiritual Laws of Vedic Philosophy)

B.B. Puri

New Age Books

ISBN: 978-81-7822-307-0

First Indian Edition: Delhi, 2008

© Author

All rights reserved. No part of this publication may be reproduced or transmitted in any form or by any means, electronic or mechanical, including photocopying, recording, or by any information storage and retrieval system, without permission in writing from the publishers.

Published by
NEW AGE BOOKS
A-44, Naraina Industrial Area, Phase-I
New Delhi 110 028 (INDIA)
Email: nab@vsnl.in
Website: www.newagebooksindia.com

Printed in India
at Shri Jainendra Press
A-45, Naraina Industrial Area, Phase-I, New Delhi 110 028

Acknowledgements

I wish to express my heartfelt thanks to all my readers for their wholehearted encouragement and support for my previous books. Their appreciation and unstinted encouragement has gone a long way in inspiring me to write this book.

My heartfelt gratitude to H.H. Swami Chidanand Saraswatiji, President Parmarth Niketan, Rishikesh, for his special blessings and guidance for completion of this book.

I also thank Ms. Madhura Karki, Asst. Dean, Tribhuvan University, Kathmandu, Nepal and Dame Prof. Dr. Meher Master Moos, President Zoroastrian College, Mumbai for their continuing promotion of Vastu Shastra by organising my lectures in the University and College.

My thanks to CPWD Training Institute, Government of India and Advanced Level Telecom Training Centre, Government of India, for regularly organising my lectures in their institutions.

I am indebted to Padmashri Dr. S. K. Sama, Chairman, World Academy of Spiritual Sciences (WASS), Sir Ganga Ram Hospital, New Delhi for his wholehearted support, and also writing a very impressive Foreword.

I wish to give my blessings to the noble soul, Miss Coralie Felicitas Srivastava, M. Phil., for taking special interest and pains in the composition and editing of the manuscript and conceptualising the computerised diagrams for this book.

Last but not the least, I offer my sincere thanks to Shri S. S. Gandhi and all my clients and friends who have faith in the Vedas, my students, staff, faculty of Vastu Research Centre and Design Gurukul and all the members of The Institution of Vastu Science (India), Research Institute of Vedic Culture and the World Academy of Spiritual Sciences, (WASS)

I would be failing in my duty if I do not express my heartfelt thanks to the life members and Board of Trustees of Research Institute of Vedic Culture, Vedic Cultural Fellowship, New Mexico, USA for their unstinted co-operation and support.

B.B. Puri

Foreword

World Health Organisation (WHO) defines healthy body, mind and soul. Medical Science also recognizes that many diseases are produced by stress, anxiety, worry and fear. There is an increasing incidence of stress related diseases in India like Coronary Artery Disease (Heart Attack), Cerebra vascular disease like cerebral strokes due to hammerage in one of the blood vessels in the brain, hypertension, diabetes etc. the Medical Science can only manage these diseases with tremendous cost to the patient or the ex-chequer. The only method of preventing these diseases and ensuring perfect heath is healthy lifestyle based on ancient Vedic Philosophy of peaceful and blissful living.

Various techniques of the art of blissful living by positive thoughts, love gratitude and compassion towards everyone and acceptance of whatever life offers, Yoga, meditation, healthy diet, rich in fruits and vegetables (Satvik Diet) as described in our Vedic Philosophy have been well illustrated in **Prof. Dr. B. B. Puri's** book on **"The Art of Blissful Living"**. I am sure, all the readers will benefit from this book and learn to be peaceful and compassionate and radiate the same to the people around them, in the house, in the community and at the place of work.

The only way that peace can prevail in the world is to work for our essential comforts of life, being peaceful within oneself and loving to other fellow beings.

I wish Dr. Puri a great success in spreading Vedic way of life through his book **" THE ART OF BLISSFUL LIVING"**.

DR. S.K. SAMA

Preface

It gives me immense pleasure in presenting to you my latest book titled *The Art of Blissful Living*.

I hope that the experiences, learning and practical tips which I have accumulated over the past years would help you in opening your mind to rediscover your inner self, to investigate, analyse and realise the very essence of life.

Living a contented life is an art, a skill, and a technique which all of us need to learn and master in order to achieve mental peace and harmony.

This book may help you in creating and maintaining a proper balance between body, mind, soul, intellect and the environment around you in line with the five elements of Nature. You will be able to reduce the stress and strain of materialistic life, leading to a state of ultimate liberation and bliss.

The tips given in the various chapters offer a practical way of life which satisfies your spiritual needs leading to mental peace along with material prosperity.

Your very self is an ocean with a fortune of undiscovered wealth and unbounded love deep inside you that you can offer to others. Your mind is so powerful that you can create an environment of your own choice to surround you.

May this book enlighten your intellect and environment, so that you can enjoy healthy, peaceful and comfortable living within the Laws of Nature.

Contents

	Acknowledgements	*v*
	Foreword	*vii*
	Preface	*ix*
	Introduction	*xiii*
1	Spiritual Laws of Vedic Knowledge	1
2	Learning Through Vedas	15
3	The Role of Vedic Culture to Enjoy Beneficial Living	29
4	The Five Elements and their Scientific Application for Blissful Living	45
5	The Mind	55
6	Mantra, Yantra and Tantra	61
7	A Remedial Measure	65
8	The Science and Art of Living	73
9	Sunlight & Sun Rays - Sustainer of Healthy Life	79
10	The Use of Ultraviolet Light & Infrared Rays for Modern, Healthy Living	89
11	How to use Ultraviolet Light, the Gift of Nature, for Our Perfect Health	97
12	Energies from Colours and Light (Influence the Mind, Body and Environment Around Us)	101
13	Rhythm of Life with Changing Colours	111
14	Vedic Vastu	117
15	Practical Vastu Tips and Simple Remedies for a Healthy Environment	125
16	The Nectar of Life (Water Therapy)	141
17	Adopting the Vedic Culture	147
18	The Magical Gift of Yoga and Meditation	153
	Conclusion	167

Introduction

My previous books titled *Vedic Architecture and Art of Living* and *Applied Vastu Shastra in Modern Architecture* have been well received by the readers. While releasing the book in a function held at Rashtrapati Bhawan on 26th December, 1995, His Excellency, Dr Shankar Dayal Sharma, The Hon'ble President of India, was all praise for the book. Doordarshan and the print media covered the event extensively.

Earlier, at the presentation Function at Jubilee Hall, Hyderabad, Smt. Vimla Sharma, First Lady of India, presented the book to Smt. Urmila Ben Patel, the then Hon'ble Union Minister for Power in the presence of Smt. Suman Krishna Kant, the First Lady of Andhra Pradesh, Shri Krishna Kant, Hon'ble Governor of Andhra Pradesh, Shri Chandra Babu Naidu, Hon'ble Chief Minister of Andhra Pradesh and Shri Mallikarjun, Hon'ble Minister for Defence and Railways.

While I was working on the 3rd Volume, a number of my students and clients encouraged me to write on the ways and means to attain peace of mind and tranquility.

The overwhelming response and encouragement to my endeavours has prompted me to present to you the third Volume on the subject entitled *A Practical Guide to an Ageless Mind*.

While man's physical structure has remained unchanged, his thought processes, his mind-sets, his living standards and his environment have undergone a sea change. Mankind, through a process of trial and error, has discovered the importance of Vastu Shastra for improving the living conditions in his abode for deriving peace of mind, health, tranquility and prosperity.

Vastu also guides us on how to live in harmony with our surroundings by rearranging the interiors in a house without making any structural changes.

This book contains practical tips and advice on how Vastu Shastra guides us in creating a healthy and harmonious living and working environment.

The book, *The Art of Blissful Living* gives very traditional (Paramparik), but convincing explanations to establish that Nature, Man and their combined products are governed by an evolutionary Network guided by Performance Standards and common sense. Vedic Knowledge is not a matter of Research. We are attempting to carry out research, but are ignorant of our basic senses! We need to accept the fact that ultimately, perfect knowledge stems from the learnings enumerated in the following quote from the *'Bhagwad Gita'*:

> I was born in the darkest ignorance, and my spiritual master opened my eyes with the touch of knowledge.

During the course of my forty years of professional experience as an Architect and Vastu Advisor, I have had many opportunities in India and abroad to study and deal with people having diverse cultural and social styles of modern living. I have been privy to the problems faced by them with respect to their factory, business establishment, commercial premises, offices, workhouses, homes, etc. I have endeavoured to discuss some of these practical issues in this book. I have also kept in view the demands made at various International Conferences by the western people to know more about the Indian philosophy, with particular reference to Vedic Science and their application to Modern Living standards.

During the course of my studies and my professional life, I have always taken a keen interest in ancestral culture and habitat, particularly those of the most ancient Vedic Period. It has been fascinating to dig out valuable data, which proves that the living style of our ancestors was really scientific and in accordance with Vedic Principles. A lot of research work has been put in to ascertain as to how Vedic Culture could be applied to our modern living to enjoy beneficial and healthy living.

The rise of Vedic Knowledge and its subsequent applications in later periods has been taken into account. The author does not wish to go into the controversy of the exact period of the Vedic Age. Indian culture and civilisation are basically spiritual in nature.

"Na pranena na apranena martyo jivati Kaschana, Itarena tu jivanti yasmin etavapasritau."

Meaning:- Our life system is not dependant merely on the process of breathing. The intake of diet is indeed important for health, but health does not rest on food alone. The entire system can be thrown out of gear if the mind is upset. A mild turbulence injected into the mind is enough to disturb the entire balance of personality. Your strength is in you. Religion begins where science ends; the beginning of the higher wisdom.

Accomplishment of Vedic Gyaan includes development of a relationship between the 'situation', namely our surroundings, climate, landform, view, topography, lights and its manifestations, colours etc., and the 'medium': material and construction techniques.

Design is a learning process. Man, his surroundings and the methods used are integral to each other and therefore, any design action is relative and requires the application of holistic, meditative and creative processes.

Similarly, nature, man and product are within an evolutionary network guided by performance standards. Vedic Culture is to be seen, felt, perceived, conceived and experienced from inside as well as from outside. It has to have a fourth dimension. However, it is essential to go into a very deep and careful study to understand its implications.

When we talk about Vedas, we are talking about knowledge. Vedas means knowledge. The mind possesses knowledge, therefore, the mind is the main author of all our actions and behaviour.

Human Beings take birth on this planet based on the composition of the five elements of nature. We take birth with five senses, but it is essential to develop these five senses through knowledge. Knowledge comes from the Vedas and Development comes from the mind.

We may possess the best knowledge, but the use of this knowledge is not through Karmas (action). It is our mind which assimilates this knowledge and puts it to the proper use.

In other words, the mind is the author, the principal, the thinker, the planner, the subject as well as the object, behind all our actions. If so, why not discuss about the mind, with the mind, for the mind. The mind that is ageless and requires no rest.

As we gain experience and advance in age, our body becomes old and weak, but our mind matures as age advances. I, therefore, decided to pen down my experiences with the aid of Vedic Knowledge. This book is a practical guide to attain an ageless mind, with the help of the spiritual laws of Vedic Knowledge and derive the benefits through the art of blissful living.

The basic reason which has prompted me to take up this book is that I have been receiving numerous letters and enquiries on a daily basis from people who are seemingly confused about which is right and which is wrong while applying the Principles of Vedic Culture. The recent profusion of articles and books available on the subject of Vedic Culture in the market has added to the confusion with contradictory information rather than providing a solution to the problem.

This state of affairs coupled with the tremendous faith vested in me by people around me has motivated me in making an attempt at clarifying to my readers some practical points which will help them to understand how and where to apply the Principles of Vedic Culture.

I was also keen to find answers to the question as to why there is this sudden, overwhelming interest in ancient Vedic Knowledge not only in India, but all over the world.

This compilation is an humble attempt to discover the synchronisation of Vedic Knowledge with Vastu Shastra.

Introduction

Present-day life in the 21st Century has become complicated, illogical and contradictory. Any attempt to describe this period fully would run into volumes, yet the end would still be nowhere in sight!

I have attempted to take a microscopic section from the magnificent Vedic period based on 'Truth' and scientific reason to show how close people are to nature and how they could learn the art of meaningful and fruitful living aided by Vedic knowledge to enjoy the gift of nature.

I am aware of the difficulties and limitations set in the path of any enterprise to seek learning from the Vedas and Upanishads. Such a venture, despite best efforts, cannot claim to be a comprehensive study of such a vast ocean of knowledge. Our aim has to be the discovery of the 'Truth' and in order to attain this goal, we must apply our minds fearlessly and without prejudice or preconception and formulate our conclusions on the basis of available evidence as far as they permit us to do so. To achieve the desired benefit in true spirit, great care is to be taken to distinguish clearly the 'Known' from the 'unknown' and to approach the 'Unmanifest' from 'Manifest'.

Vedas regulate the relation between man and his environments. A learner should exhibit his skill by overcoming the difficulties and differences between the principles laid down in the 'Vedas' and the need of the present-day requirements, keeping in mind the original relation between man and nature and to find acceptable solutions. For good results it is all the more important to put the correct question rather than to find the correct answers to the wrong questions.

We have to create harmony between the common values, moral codes, individual beliefs, ideological convictions, economic conditions, social obligations and cultural symbolisations coupled with philosophical ideas and meaningful environment. During the Vedic period, people built homes, temples and hermitages not merely to be used as shelter but mainly with a view to having a peaceful place for offering prayers, find peace and to live in common harmony. The ancient philosophic concept represents two different logical processes – the 'Inductive' and 'Deductive'. The former took its stand upon 'Smriti' or reasoned knowledge and law of cause and effect and the latter dependent upon insight or inspiration, known as 'Shruti' or divine revelation of which the Vedas are said to be the expression. In modern language we may call these as an objective or atheistic and subjective or theistic science towards the finer and subtler aspects of life and consciousness.

One ponders over answers to vital questions like: What was the beginning ? How does the Universe evolve? What is the real constitution of a human being? What is the ultimate? etc. The Vedas proclaim that the consciousness, the Universal Will, the Omnipresent and the Omnipotent 'Brahma' (Purusha) is without beginning or end. The 'Eternal' contains Space (Akash), Time (Kala), Energy (Pran) and Nature (Prakriti). The all-pervading consciousness regulates the entire cosmos and illuminates or gives a spark of life to all individual beings. Death and decay are the source of new creation.

The Vedas propound that apart from the physical body; an individual constitutes his mind and his intellect and is presided over or enlivened by the Cosmic Consciousness. The mind function is two fold, to acquire knowledge through the five senses (Gyan Indrias) and to act in the world outside through the five related organs (Karam Indrias). The five basic elements of nature, namely, the space, air, fire, water and earth correspond to the sensations of hearing, touch, sight, taste and smell, respectively. Intellect is the discriminating power in us, to take a decision for elevation to righteousness or to indulge in sensual short-lived pleasures; to endeavour to rediscover alpha and omega of the Reality or to succumb to desires and remain in worldly illusions.

Our existence comprises of three stages of awareness: waking, dream and deep sleep stages. We also have three behavioural qualities: 'Satvic', 'Rajas' and 'Tamas'; *i.e.* spiritual, psychological or merely physical ways of living. We are taught that by knowledge, selfless service and by meditation we can achieve the ultimate. Knowledge can be derived from 'Yantras', creativity from 'Tantras', energies from 'Mantras' and inspiration from 'Meditation'; the secret laws of nature.

I have combined all these together in Vedic Culture to achieve best results. Despite materialistic development, resources and riches, the Westerners are looking to the orient for desired peace of mind.

An open secret, relatively unknown, is that India is a source, the fountainhead of the vast ancient Vedic knowledge available on the planet today. When the Vedic concept is presented through modern technological advances, the sublime information becomes available to all walks of life and can be easily understood. This would give a new outlook to the world of modern living with high thinking.

Scientific explanations and Sanskrit Shlokas with their meaning, wherever possible, have been inducted to project the genuineness of the subject.

This is an humble attempt in giving a glimpse of habitation and the way of life in ancient India. As far as possible, my submission on the inter-relationship of the Vedic Knowledge vis-a-vis modern living in unison with nature as expounded in the vedic age are supported by diagrams, charts, illustrations and photographs.

Last of all I would like to stress that :

> If we have to equip ourselves to meet the challenges of the future, we must examine the forces that are now transforming the living activity and thoughts of the people. However, in the modern world people built concrete clusters mainly for high rate of return. After the second world war, the architectural practice must have turned out to be a race towards the so called modernisation, adopting bureaucratic values, resulting in world wide pollution, environmental and ecological problems with no peace of mind under any kind of shelter.

Sanskrit Shloka

Sukham Dhanani Budhimsch Santati Servadanrinam I
Priyanesham ch Sansidhim Servasyat Shubhlaxanam II

Yatra Nindit laxmatra tahitesham vidhakrit I
Athservamupadeyam Yabhdavet Shubhlaxanam II
Deshah purniwashch Sabhavisam Sanani Ch I
Yadyadidrisamanyashch Tathashreyaskaram Matam II
Vastusahstradritetasya Na Syallaxannirnayah I
Tasmat Lokasya Kripya satmetbhaduriyate II

Meaning:- Properly designed and pleasing house will be an abode of good health, wealth, family, peace and happiness. Negligence of the canons of Vastu Principles will result in bad name, loss of fame, sorrow and disappointments. Vastu Shastra is, therefore, brought into light in favour of, to the satisfaction of, and for the betterment and overall peace and welfare of the Universe.

Veda's are the foundation of civilisation and if the foundation is not correct, good results can never be achieved. Vastu is our heritage. Heritage is like roots to a tree. So we have to go to the roots and study the most elementary and important principles of Vedas for a healthier and prosperous life, particularly in modern living. The goal of the discourses is to successfully harness the resources of heritage and give strength to the individual and thereby to the community as a whole.

The Vastu Professional should know Vedas. He should be intellectually aware of the highest truth formulated in religion. The subject of Vastu Shastra is one among several sacred sciences derived from the highest metaphysical principles. The Vastu practitioner should put in sincere efforts to acquire this comprehensive, farsighted and timeless wisdom. Research Institute of Vedic Culture has been established to give answers to all the questions. The students and scholars of this institution are busy doing their Research Thesis on Vedic Culture and Occult Sciences.

In the 3rd edition of this book I would like to discuss with the readers the importance of orientation of a building not only for saving energy but also to have a healthy design, which not only gives comfortable living but also gives good health, prosperity to the house owners/ occupiers and their families.

Introduction

There lies a correlation between the rotational scenario of the planets and the house designs and their different activities in the house placed in different directions with respect to the North. The science dealing with sunshine and the effects of its intensity per given area, its rotation around the sun, earth tilt at 23 ½ degree towards the sun, Earth's attraction by the moon coupled with its environs, as its meteorological data, sea behaviour, ice caps in NORTH and SOUTH poles, rainfall, soil data, space track of the earth etc. has to be referred and studied deeply to understand the effects on human mind, body and soul in relation with the building and its environments and surrounding.

During the Vedic period, man had discovered how to utilise and improve upon the living conditions of his habitat for perpetual prosperity with the help of Vastu Shastra as described in the 'YAJURVEDA'. The Vedic principles dealing in building designs and construction existed before the Mahabharata, and had been practised by our ancient architects like Vishvakarama, such a wide variety that could be achieved only by collaboration and integration with the most modern high technology of building sciences fused with vedic sciences. A glimpse into the Vedic Sciences has been described and dealt in depth by the same author in his earlier book titled *Vedic Architecture and Art of Living*-volume I.

The Greatest Discovery Of Mankind Is That A Human Being Can Change, Alter Or Mould His Life By Altering His Attitude Through His Trained Mind.

B.B. Puri

–1–
Spiritual Laws of Vedic Knowledge

The Vedas are a systematic and formulated source of knowledge that explains the relationship between Man, Nature and God.

The Vedas train us to think for ourselves and to rediscover oneself, to analyse, investigate and realise the very essence of life. Living a contented life is an art, a skill, a technique which all of us need to learn and master if we are to achieve mental peace and harmony.

The Vedas help us in creating and maintaining a proper balance between body, mind, intellect and the five elements of nature. They help us in reducing the stress and strain of materialistic living, leading to a state of ultimate liberation and Bliss.

Your very self is an ocean with a fortune of undiscovered wealth deep inside and unbounded love that you can offer to others. Your mind is so powerful that you can create an environment of your own choice to surround you.

Let us all be true seekers and devote ourselves to reach the state of ultimate bliss and liberation.

Health and Happiness are not by chance... They have to be chosen.

The Vedas offer us a practical way of life which satisfies our Spiritual and Mental Peace along with material prosperity.

God gives what we NEED and not necessarily what we think we WANT or DESIRE. What man really needs is Knowledge, Love and Service.

The Science and Philosophy of the Vedas is the answer to the urgent needs of mankind.

It is a misconception that 'nature' is hostile to man. If approached in true harmony, its secrets can be revealed and the energies harnessed for the benefit of the living beings. But any relation of the competition and conquest is not only productive but ultimately leads to environment and ecological disparities, which is 'unnatural'.

The ancient philosophic concepts represented two different logical processes—the inductive and deductive. The former took its stand upon 'Smriti' or reasoned knowledge and the law of cause and effect and the latter depended upon insight or inspiration, known as 'Shruti' or divine revelation, of which the Vedas are said to be the highest expression. In the modern language, we may call these as objective or atheistic science and subjective or theistic science towards the finer and more subtle aspects of life and consciousness.

The specialist approach of the objective sciences has developed during the last three hundred years of the scientific and industrial revolution and the post-war (1945) management and information development. The scope of research is strictly within the physical phenomena. (Incidentally, one finds these developments in the cold regions of the world where absolute physical survival is of critical priority for life to sustain and manifest. Nature is hostile to man and the man-nature relations are of competition and conquest.)

In the holistic approach, the physical and metaphysical, theistic and atheistic man, environment, objectives, mediums, tools are all considered as inseparable whole, because each is a part of, and a cause of, the evolutionary process of this great act of cosmic creative cycle. Here too, one finds clear scope and 'thresholds' of specialised fields, but, at all the scales, the central theme is holistic, and one is constantly reminded of being 'the part within the part, the whole around the whole, the universe within the universe concept. The context of CONSCIOUSNESS, LIFE and MAN are complementary, constant and central. This is also 'subtropical science'. (One finds this culture developed around the tropical and subtropical valleys, where physical survival was not critical due to friendly Eco-cultural relationships. Evolution of mind and spirit take natural priority. The physical does not pose apparent limitations for life and living. It only remains an essential base from where one takes off the journey towards the finer and more subtle aspects of life and consciousness).

These are various thought processes. There was further development into Puranas. Arts, sciences and technologies also developed to highly refined levels. Vedic Mathematics, astronomy, astrology, arts, literature, music, dance, sculpture, painting, ayurveda, vastu shastra, yoga, naturopathy, metallurgy, etc. also developed to similar levels. (Interestingly, development of long span structures did not catch attention, probably because the local weather did not need these.)These are the major processes of the vedic creations.

EVOLUTION

One ponders to find answers to vital questions like:

> What was the beginning of the beginning? (PURUSHA)- Man
> How did all these evolve?(PRAKRITI)-Nature
> How can one say relevant from irrelevant?
> What is the ultimate?

There are many questions the 'atheists' and the 'rationalists' are equally interested. Both have theories. And, the important ones are also parallel. But many questions remain unanswered. Also, the Paradox is that the more one is informed, the less he knows! If there was 'nothing' before the beginning, how did anything begin? (A big theory)

The Vedas say:

The Vedas proclaim that Consciousness, the universal Will, is without Beginning or End. Paramatman. The Eternal contains space(Akash), Energy(Prana), Mass(Rayi), Time(Kala), Movements (Gati), Transformation (parivertan), Atma – Purusha(Individual consciousness) and Nature(Prakriti). This word of names and forms.)

The all-pervading consciousness regulates the entire cosmos and illumines or gives spark of life to all individual beings. Death and decay are the source of new creation. Ref. Diag 1 Cycle of life

There is the law of creation, the law of maintenance and evolution and the law of dissolution. Briefly, the rudiments of Vedantic thoughts can be depicted in 'Trimurti', namely,

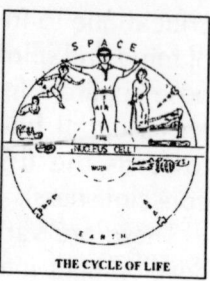

Diag. 1

Diag. 2

'Brahma', The Creator; 'Vishnu', The Sustainer; and 'Mahesh', The Annihilator Ref Diag 2 Trimurti.

The Universe is governed by the positive laws with innumerable names and forms, constantly changing, moving and transforming. Ever fresh, even death and destruction are the source of new creations: Time, movements, transformations, informations, thoughts, creation, destruction exist ever since. Like design exists ever since.

The mind is the unique creation of the Great Designer. To enjoy this grand play of consciousness, the Leela of Purusha and Prakriti, one has to observe it, discover it, create out of it and merge into it again.

The 'Adwaitas' call this a singular play of consciousness. The 'Dwaitas' call this the dance grand outs between the Mind and Consciousness call. This is the game of creation.

The Vedantic knowledge process insists on reminding constantly to the following principles in the form of peace invocation chanted before starting every lesson. This deals with the holistic attitude, the other with the need to constantly work together as a team.

SHLOKA

Purnamadah Purnamidam Purnat purnam Udachyate,
Purnasya Purnamadaya, Purnameva Vashishyate

Meaning :- This is perfect, that is perfect and from the perfect, the perfect emerges. If perfect is deducted from the perfect only the perfect remains.

SHLOKA

"Sahanavavtu Sahanabhunkty Sahaveeryam Karavavahai, Tejeswina Wadhitamastu ma Vidvishavahai om, shanti, shanti,shanti!"

Meaning :- Let Him protect us both, We be blessed with the bliss of knowledge, Let us do the brave act together, May our studies be thorough and faithful, May we not ever misunderstand each other, Oh: Eternity: Peace: Peace: Peace.

The last two lines are a warning towards the possible lack of accuracy and thoroughness of 'the Generalist'. Also, the lack of communication results in misunderstanding or misapplication of information or knowledge to design. Thorough understanding, right application and meaningful communication are important. To get a perfect result it is better to put correct question than to give correct answer to a wrong question.

According to the Upanishads, a human has five senses and super human intellectual man can open his sixth sense, called 'The Third Eye of Cosmic Vision'.

The perfect Man consists of 16 Kalas, 3 states of awareness and 3 states of behavioural qualities. 1. Prana; 2 Faith; 3. Akasha; 4. Air; 5. Fire; 6. Water; 7. earth; 8. the senses; 9. Mind; 10. food; 11. strength; 12 Thought; 13. Mantra; 14. Karma; 15. the world; 16. Names.

Three awareness states are: Awake, Dream and Sleep. Three behavioural states are Tamas, Rajas and Satva.

Man, above all, is a tool making instrument. He communicates and expands beyond his physical frame through mind, spirit, smell and instrumentation. This quality of man needs to be guided for positive co-existence. His various faculties be trained and disciplined for the highest efficiency, positive co-existence and creative efforts.

Now, let us understand the Nature, Man and Vedas transfer process. If man is the reflection of Nature, Vedas reflect man and his total personality. Human body and mind complex are instruments which communicate, expand and get consumed in the nature. Nature, Man and Vedas are the natural evolutionary extensions of one another, forming a complete whole.

DIAG. 3 VASTU KALA GRAPHIC SYMBOLS FOR UNIVERSAL DESIGN SPIRITUAL LAWS OF EARTH, WATER, AIR, FIRE(SUN) AND SPACE

Man is the subject, object and cause of knowledge in relation to his experience of himself with the surrounding world. As a tool making animal, he designs and controls his environment and buildings. They, by the environmental changes created by him to suit his choices of living, directly reflect his personal, social, material, emotional, intellectual and vital personalities.

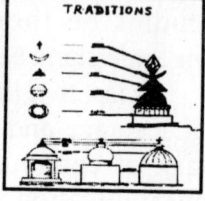

Diag. 3

Through the act of design, he alters and moulds the elements of natural environment. The sequences of the natural elements when used as 'The Mediums' or 'The Materials' of knowledge reverse as follows:

Earth, Water, Air, Sun and Space.(From Physical to ethereal). Earth and Water have limited and localised availability for human habitat and growth. Since earth and water have cognisable physical body, they form apparent and fundamental choice makers in the location and the physical form of Vastu Kala habitat. Though Sun, Air and Space also form select priorities for comfortable human life, apparently these are universally available and can be moulded to human needs by the act of design by earth and water. Among all these, water is shy element. Habitat, therefore, goes where water is. Only in some very special situations, water is diverted to habitat. But this decision is often expensive and unfeasible, economically and ecologically.

Ideal habitats, cultures, healthy environment and Vastu Shastra and life have naturally shown exhilarance where all the five physical elements to support life are abundantly available and are suitable to human growth and evolution. The oldest, the rich and the living cultures and civilisations all over the globe have been along the temperate zones, i.e., the Zone of Cancer and the Zone of Capricorn, where the evolution of human mind reached its peak at the earliest. The recorded period of the present history goes back to 5000 years, when one knows that about 4000 years ago, in these regions, the human super minds lived. In other regions, such as, Equator or the colder regions, civilisations and cultures developed later. In order to understand the act to design with these five physical elements we shall take each one separately to appreciate their meaning, role and workability. For the present, broadly, they form their scope for human habitat as follows:

Earth:- Mother Land gives us productivity, food, vegetables, fruits. Land Structure, Landform, Landscape, Flora and Fauna. It also establishes availability of local construction materials and their workability. Recycling.

Water:- The habitat and physical life are, where water is. This is true for all life forms and Eco-cultures. The type, form and pattern of life also greatly depend on relationship of earth and water. The sea front, river front, lake front, the underground water level or streams for wells are also important for flora to grow. Water is not the only life source, but is surely fundamental to location and growth of habitats.

Air:- As a life supporting element, air is very powerful life source. Two minutes of blockage of air supply to respiratory system can smoothen life. Pure air with oxygen is good for brain and blood. Human physical comfort values are directly and sensitively dependent on correct humidity, air flow, temperature of air, air pressure, air composition and its content. In this respect, air deals with the entire body surface through skin, respiratory and blood system through respiration. Building systems, to handle air for comfort conditions, have direct impact on the form and visual qualities of habitats. Air also represents movement and climatic condition and weather change.

Fire (Sun):- A source of mental energy. Best minds evolve in a natural process where the sun was temperate. Not very hot, not very cold, just the right temperature (+or−3⁰) of 24 degree Celsius. The hot sun has glare, sharp light and dark shadows. Cool sun has colours and cold sun rarely rises above horizon or often geographically coupled with heavy clouds in the sky and snow on earth. Generally gloomy but beautiful, silvery and long hours of twilight. Hot humid zones with heavy cloudy sky for longer periods of the year also have distinctive culture. Sun has played an important role in the development of visual qualities of vastu kala. In terms of textures, colours, roof firms, and, above all, expressions of vitality 80% of body energy comes from sun.

Space: All the above elements are skillfully engineered towards the creation of physically comfortable, emotionally pleasant, intellectually determinant, totally vibrant and blissfully satisfying spaces for human shelter and habitat. Man lives in Space.

The main Vastu Shastra rule for planning is orientation. All the Cosmic Rays, nine planets (Navgrah) are the source from the Space.

The Vedic concept describes the creation in two basic phenomena: Purusha and Prakriti.

Purusha is consciousness, the life source. It is also called Atman. The Paramatman or Vaishwanara (the universal consciousness), the Atman (Individual consciousness), Prana (life) and jiva (also life or soul). Atman reflects as Prana or jiva in the body through mind. Purusha is timeless, ageless, constant, absolute consciousness. A singular truth–Adwaita. Prana is the central source of all energies in all living things, and not energy itself. Prakriti is the world of name and forms:

ever changing, evolving and operating in Dwaita. The dualism of positive or negative, creations or destruction, good–bad, male–female etc.

Prakriti has countless forms. The Prakriti also has permanence, but of different nature. It is in the cyclic relay order *i.e.* while the species survives over the time, the body of the species is created and destroyed and recreated again and again. So, at a given body level it is temporary. After Prakriti comes Purusha, the life source. Purusha manifests itself in Prakriti through Ego and Ambition. Thus the Purusha is the life, essence, the idea, the will behind any name from the physical world. In the absence of which the physical mass, forms or system simply crumble and decompose. Purusha is the power behind all physical existence.

THE MIND

Mind is the Lord and author of man's physical world around. The mind mainly operates at two levels. The external (convex) mind receives and reflects all information from the Prakriti (The external world of names and forms). The physical world consists of five elements; Space, Air, Water, Fire and Earth. These represent Sound, Touch, Taste, Sight and Smell. Thus, the mind may be fed informations as per the 'interests' or conditioning of the sense organs. The objectives of sense organs are Artha, Kama and Dharma (Wealth, Comfort and Glory). The external surface of mind is in constant touch with external world and its nature to be mobile constantly, so as to efficiently perform its basic job to keep in touch with Prakriti informations and to transmit *i.e.,* to communicate the same.

This wandering mind is constantly in wants, desires, feelings of incompleteness. Always wanting, never satisfied. This makes man insecure, weak and lacking in confidence. So, man needs psychological and moral support all the time *viz.* support for any MEDIUM (*Religion, work, people, etc.*)

The core mind or the inner mind has function of communicating with Purusha. However, unlike the outer Mind, it does not depend on external physical sense instruments.

This mind has to train itself to be self operative. An untrained mind may feel this capacity at times but cannot operate at will on this facility. Unlike Prakriti, Purusha is stable, timeless, ageless, continuous, pure consciousness, source of creativity, the beginning of all beginnings, life behind all Prakriti. The inner mind is introvert, quiet and meditative, a constant source of Truth, solitude and happiness. Inner mind is made of Satvika aspects of the five elements and sheaths (physical, emotional, intellectual, vital energy and bliss). Its goal is to seek communication between Atman and Paramatman and to merge it with Paramatman when detached from the mind-body complex. This mind never dies and has continuity with time and space. The informations collected, stored and processed by individual minds get transmitted to the universal over a large geographical region.

Human Problems

The human problems are of three kinds:

1. Two basic human desires: To procure the desired and to protect the procured. This is the constant source of the feelings of insecurity (Ambition-Rajas)
2. If he can manage, he would wish to have it with no effort or minimum effort (Tamas).
3. The restless external mind is, time and again, reminded by the inner mind to hold, think, meditate, come back to the self, co-operate with the Purusha in the law of Prakriti. There is a constant struggle within the mind.

Patanjali's Yoga Sutra

As solution to the above problems, various answers or the viewpoints have evolved, called Darshanas. The Yoga Sutra avoids external mediums as far as possible (though does not bar them) and has developed Yoga technology and attitudes with the Mind-Body complex itself as medium and auto-suggestive methods. The schools are of little relevance for the purpose of evolving patterns for architectural expressions.

However, it is mentioned for its importance in training of the designers creative mental attitudes.

The Icons, Yantras and Mandalas

These are of visual responses or codes. These are visual symbols as mediums or invocation, Icons or Murti or Statues in human forms, semi-human, animal or demonic forms. These are most popular among the visual symbols for the common people. The iconic symbols range from a human figure representing the entire universe (Vaishvanara, Viratswarupa, etc.) to various other specific energy systems to be invoked for a particular objective such as Shakti, Lakshmi, Saraswati, Brahma, Vishnu, Shiva etc. Each one with specific symbols is associated to represent the energies assimilated within the specific network.

Knowledge to Design or Create

Through understanding, right application and meaningful communication are important team work. In order to keep the total balance, it has to be very accurate.

For any activity following are the three aspects :-

1. Mantra or concept (energy)
2. Yantra or mediums (instruments or tools)
3. Tantra or act of creation (administration)

1. *The Mantra or Concept*

Mantras are graphic symbols representing the respective energy networks. Each Yantra has its mantra as well as icon. Shri Mantra, Gayatri Mantra, Surya, Yogini, Vishnu etc. All Yantras evolve patterns from a central point. This centre is considered the source of creation and the object for concentration. The concentric patterns around the centre are specific to the energy pattern one wishes to invoke. This pattern is visual code to constantly remind the sadhaka of the network he is meditating on.

These are for audial response or codes. It may be monosyllable like OM, Rim, Klim, Fat, etc. or in hymn form with the combination of sounds, words, dictions of specific composition to invoke a given set of energies.

2. Yantra or Mediums

Yantras are for the intellectually superior or evolved persons who may not need icons. Yantras are generally two dimensional, symmetric, concentric patterns using elementary geometric forms such as circle, square and other regular geometric polygons. Lotus flowers varying from four to one hundred petals are also incorporated. Yantra can be designed and developed to represent any specific energy network. Yantras have colour codes too.

3. Tantra or Act of Creation

The problem is of the relationships between the sense organs and the external mind. The mind and the sense both should be disciplined and be in harmony and awareness with Prana. Mediums and methods are developed responding to senses and the sensuality of mind. First the mind should have positive reasons and clear objectives to concentrate upon.

To reach that state of stability some intermediary mediums: vehicles or catalysts–are developed. These carriers are sound, touch, vision, taste and smell, since these are the factors of sense organs the mediums or vehicles should correlate with the specific objectives. It should have potency to reach the goal and its directions and action network to be with clear accurate commands. Mantras, Yantras and Tantras are developed with these considerations. In Sanskrit these are defined as:

Protection through mind is Mantra Sound (concept)
Protection through effort is Yantra Karma (work)
Protection through crossing (hurdles) is Tantra (management and methods)

Mantra is for mental conceptual efficiency. Sound (Audial Form) is its vehicle.

Yantra is for work efficiency. Vision (visual form) is its vehicle.

Tantra is for management efficiency. Process is its vehicle.

Similarly, there are specific touch, taste and smells associated with specific Mantra, Yantra and Tantra.

The above three are MEDIUM and METHODS bridging human WILL to objectives, designed and developed for various kinds of human desires, Material, Emotional, Intellectual, Vital Bliss.

Tamasika, Rajasika or Satvika. While these mediums are used to help a Sadhaka to attain initial meditation practice, these are more popular among the common people as methods to attain material goals of life. For the second group of goals, one is interested in satisfying certain specific desires such as procure and protect, wealth, comforts, glory sensual or mental gratifications, etc. For each of these the MEDIUMS are utilised to invoke specific set of energies in a desired pattern of network and potency.

GOD REALISATION

"That which permeates all, which nothing transcends and which, like the universal space around us, fills everything completely from within and without, that supreme non-dual brahman-that thou art."

Shankaracharya

–2–
Learning Through Vedas

The God (PRAKRITI) principle or universal Truth/consciousness has no beginning, no end, is formless, beyond time and space, all pervading, all powerful, eternal, omnipresent, infinite, manifest and unmanifest, beyond expression in words!

- God is a circle whose centre is everywhere and whose circumference is infinity. He is the reality in everything.
- God is nearer to me than I am to myself. I feel God's presence in every breath.
- God is love and love is God—everything is God. He is one in all—all in one.
- To see / know God is to be God. Self-realisation is the realisation of God.
- Do not go into the history of God but go into his mystery.
- Know the truth and the truth shall make you free.
- He who rests in the Lord, dwells in bliss forever.
- Practice of seeing God in all things, confers immediate experience of bliss on the aspirant.
- Without devotion and consequent grace of the Master, man's endeavour is in vain.

O Lord! Bless me that my thoughts and actions become an offering unto Thee—may Thou be my unseen companion in all my ways of living.

GYAAN YOG

He is the living Master who having himself realised the 'sat' (truth) and Godhood, is 'Samarth' (capable) of leading aspirants

/Sadhaks to salvation. The Sadhak has to have complete 'Shradha' (devotion) and surrender his ego (body, mind and sense of possession) and to follow, in word and spirit, the teachings of the Satguru.

The Master sees through the mind of the devotee as one sees through a crystal. He guides and leads the devotee to self-realisation. His words, acts and even a mere look may captivate one into a state of happy submission or command to a course of stern discipline.

Shloka

"Guru Brahma, Guru Vishnu, Guru Deva Maheshwara,
Guru Sakshat Paar Brahma; Tasmaye Shri Guruvai Namah"

Meaning:-'Guru Is Akin To Brahma (The Creator-Unmanifest Becoming Manifest), Vishnu (The Sustainer) And Mahesha (The Annihilator- Manifest Becoming Unmanifest)-He Is The Embodiment Of Godliness. To Such A Master, I Pay My Obeisance'.

The Master Is Like Krishna, Vashisht or Ashtavakar And The Aspirant- Sadhak Has To Be Arjun, Ram Or Janak.

"That in whom reside all beings and who is the giver of all, the supreme soul of the universe, the limitless being (sat)-I am that"- Amritbindu Upanishad

In order that you may be liberated, even when you are in this life, in order that the wide world may become a heaven for you, you will have to realise that you are nothing but a parcel of God, the divine principle, the impersonal Supreme Being. This divine'subjective'knowledge is acquired, with the grace of gyana not through the intellect but by conviction (nishchay) in the language of feeling, permeating your blood, running through your veins, throbbing with your pulse, being instilled into you. This discovery can bring renunciation, which places you at your best, enhances your powers, multiplies your energies and strengthens your force. It takes all your sorrows, anxiety and fear and you become happy. The knowledge of the 'truth', of the real 'atman', of what you are, makes you 'jeevan-mukta.

When we do not see the object but see the immutable (unchanging through time) behind all objects, when our looks do not fasten upon this object or that one, that enables our heart to see divinity or the true self in them when that stage is reached, it is easy for a man to realise the unity, the oneness with the whole world. The next higher stage will be when you are entirely merged in divinity, when you are in a stage of trance, a state of union and absorption, a state of immersion- this is the state of 'Godliness' or 'Nirvana'.

Ignite the light of wisdom. Surrender yourself to God without any ego. Allow the will of God to work through you. Feel the union of God within and accept every happening as his 'Prasads'; abide by the Master's will unconditionally.

Realisation is not a thing to be achieved. To gain Godly vision, you have simply to undo what you have already done in the way of forming dark cocoons of desire around you. Shake off vain fancies; burn up all crookedness. When the little 'I' ego's bubble bursts, it finds itself as a part of the whole ocean and not a separated drop.

RAJ YOG

A Sadhak begins to perceive that knowledge is within and he must help himself to practise the power of faith and conviction, as propounded by the Master / Satguru.

The Sadhak is immune to pain and the external events happening around him.

Freedom of the 'Chitta': He realises that all difficulties, struggles and vacillations of the mind fall down. It is the end of all actions / duty through discrimination.

"Sadhak is established in its own self, that neither body nor mind were ever related, much less attached to him. That he has been ever blessed and requires none else to make him happy, for he is happiness itself."-Brahm Nirvan

As soon as man abolishes his ego—purely, entirely to the very root—GOD alone remains and is all in all, He is all pervading. Man cannot produce GOD for himself, but he can do away with his self (EGO) as the great negation and then he passes into GOD.

We have to sublimate the Gunas and to Nirguna, to cease to dance to the tune of the 'Prakriti'. Instead making her dance to the tune of self. In short, every one of the senses of the flesh has to be turned into a 'Sense of the Spirit'. Every one of them has to be intimately related to the self which alone gives them light and life, until all the senses, the whole non-self becomes the self, even as iron, when every component of it is in contact with fire, becomes like fire.

Self does not act. He, who holds his 'WILL' at the disposal of GOD, shall ultimately reach the knowledge that his will and GOD's will are one.

'Gyan Yogi' has his eye fixed on the absolute, takes his cue from it, and turns all actions into inaction - contemplating and meditating on the impersonal absolute; the Devotee basking in the glow and warmth of His presence, His praise and His grace.

The Mind

The mind is nothing but a bundle of thoughts integrated to generate the illusory appearance of the ego or the individual. Thus, the light reflected on the mind produces both, the ego and the world. When aware of the self - why worry about these shadows?

The thought of distraction is as much a creation of the mind. To meditate is to be the 'EVER LUMINOUS' self (not like the meditation of some object to the exclusion of other thoughts) the eternal truth, reality, omnipresent, being and hence the easiest thing to do.

This Sansara (World of Appearance; Nam - Roop) is nothing but the mind filled with likes and dislikes. It is a delusion of creation. When the mind is free of such thoughts, worldly appearance too comes to an end. The inert aspect of the mind is the cause of the illusory appearance of the world, because of the omnipresence of consciousness, the mind takes the form of the knowable and thus becomes the seed of the Universe. The mind like a child imagines the existence of the world. When the mind is 'Illumined' it experiences infinite consciousness within itself.

The mind alone is the creator of the world. What is done by the mind is 'Action' while what is done by the body (without the involvement of the mind) is not an action. One whose consciousness is extroverted, experiences pleasure and pain, while the yogi whose vision is introverted, does not entertain ideas of pain and pleasure that are in reality two sides of the same coin.

The mind must recognise and penetrate its own being; turn it into an instrument of self-discovery. Avoid protracted battles with mind—just live your life as it comes, but alertly, watchfully, allowing everything to happen as it happens naturally.

Mind is a flow of thoughts, like a stream of water. It beats against rocks; it seeps through crevices, splashes and makes waves, but is always flowing. To go with the flow, to move forward against all odds, to be still when the time is right—a stream of water does all this and much more.

The individualised consciousness (mind) has its own manifold potentialities in an extremely subtle state, known as individual soul. One has to train his mind in a disciplined manner, in a creative way.

Geeta Gyan

When the author of the GEETA introduces Krishna in first person, it is the divine in Arjuna and in every one of us (Capital 'I'–Universal Consciousness) speaking to the small 'I' individual.

Krishna is in every one of us, that we would feel and act on the influence of his presence if we were purged of all passion and pride and had ceased to run after earthly things that he would listen to us only if we surrender our ego to him and seek refuge in him.

He who finds happiness only within, rests only within, feels enlightened only within, that Yogi, having become one with 'Prakriti' (Nature) attains oneness with Brahman—the seer who has mastered himself and who is engrossed in the welfare of all.

That ascetic is ever free; who, having shut out all external senses and contacts, sits with his gaze fixed between the brows, breathing in and out harmoniously; holding his senses, mind and reason in check; rid of longing, fear and wrath and intent on freedom.

To those who obey him, he will reveal himself in the toils, the conflicts, the sufferings that they shall pass through in his fellowship, and as an indescribable mystery, they shall learn in their experience who he is.

The way to the fulfilment of a desire is to give it up, renounce it and rise above it all. So long as you hanker and show hunger for it, you will never get it or reach it. The moment you renounce it, develop a mood of recklessness about it, it is presented to you the very next moment!

Happiness is within—expansion of self—the infinite in the finite. All the apparent phenomena of the dream, of the deep sleep, of the wakeful state; are mutable, changeable, fickle, uncertain and indefinite. The real self shines upon the three states and illumines your experience and the entire world, in exactly the same way as the mere presence of the Sun is seen to invoke life and activities in the outer world.

To see all things in one's own self and to see one's own self in all things; is to have a real eye, without which there can be no love or beauty attracting it. Originally, we have to realise the whole world as our body and then the same is dismissed, merged in the truth, in the self that is myself. You must pass through a stage where you find the true self permeating and pervading all names and forms.

The law is that the cross pierces the little false self. The world is a Garden of Eden to him who suffers willing crucifixtion. To all else it is a paradise lost. The law is FIRE, it burns up all worldly attachments. As to receiving response from the Lord, do not be deluded Dear! His breast instantaneously, nay, simultaneously, heaves with thy breast in responsive muscle.

Deliverance (through Knowledge) dispossesses your mind of all you have become poor and without claims, and behold, you shall be Lord and sovereign of all things.

Happy is the man who can ever feel his oneness with all, who can feel his true divinity; when he sees not the personality (Body) but the reality in the person.

"Your Faith has healed you, Not I"—said Christ.

"My precious child, I love you and would never leave you. During your trial and suffering (when you see only one set of footprints in the sand of time) I carried you in my arms"—said Christ.

The true self is not the body, neither any of the five senses or the organs of action, nor the prana nor the mind.

It is active yet free from the urge to act, inactive yet free from any self–restraint, spontaneous, effortless and therefore free, unrelated to the past or the future.

'Awareness' in which the 'I' thought is extinguished to reveal the Sat – Chit – Anand: that verily is 'Maaun' (silence) self.

If the objective vision of things seen (Drishya) disappears as illusory, the true nature of the seer, the subject, is realised.

True renunciation is giving up desires, passions and attachment. He, who renounces the immediate ties, actually extends his affection and love to the whole of creation.

For the Yogi the Lord is as the self of all-alike who considers all attachment to sensory objects as shackles that bind the ATMAN; not overtaken by grief or joy. (Samta attitude considering that everything happens by his will as impartial justice), calm, patient, full of compassion and equally loving all: having developed' Vairagya' through discrimination to the Ignorant, the 'I' is the self limit to the body: to the wise, the 'I' is the self infinite, eternal, all-pervading.

The self supreme is confined. The abnormality of life is that it is cooped up in and confined to the dungeon of flesh—this life of the ego, its corporeal existence, is really the greatest calamity, which the ego has made into a normality; an obsession to be doted upon!

The majesty of the self that transcends death is realised by one becoming free from will and desire (doership), from sorrow and delusion; and by the grace of the Lord.

Yoga, when attained, will be something indescribable, precluding all desire for other gains and joys—it shall be absolute bliss of an everlasting contact with Brahman. Such a yogi will see universal self in all beings and all beings in that self.

Bhakti Yog

It requires you to live in your family as per your prarabhdha. You are not to run away from the grahastha, you are to live in the given position as a witness and an impersonal God; not attached; in no way mixed up or entangled. All relations are mere illusions. Keep your mind fixed upon the divinity within.

Prayer is conversation with God, the language of the spirit and heart to seek communion with our higher selves through profound reflections in which our most subtle faculties are brought out.

Heaven is within you. You play the part of an impure, unchaste adulterer when you stoop down to indulge in so called external objects of pleasure.

A yogi is said to be steadfast when he puts away all the cravings that arise in his mind and finds comfort for himself from the inner atma that resides inside him.

Brooding on the objects of the senses is substituted by contemplation of the Lord: free from a sense of 'I' and 'Mine'. He refrains from claiming anything of his own. And endures the pair of opposites (likes and dislikes) which come and go and remains indifferent to pleasure or pain, cold or heat, gain or loss, victory or defeat.

KARMA YOG

To begin with, I ask you not to cry over spilt milk (The Past). It spoils our present and we also fear the future that is concealed from us by providence. Why probe into what God chooses to hide from us? You thereby create suffering for yourself. Forget the past, keep the gate shut behind you and hold no anxiety about the future. Live in the 'Present', for it is the only moment you have. It is rightly said:

> The PAST is History
> The FUTURE is a mystery
> The PRESENT is just what it is, A GIFT, make the best of it!

- Listen to your body's wisdom, the signals of comfort and discomfort.
- Take time to be silent, to meditate, to silence the internal dialogue.
- My happiness depends upon the way I meet the events of life, not on the events.
- Real renunciation is giving up that which the mind likes the most.
- No expectations means no disappointments.
- Want makes us a beggar. Everything comes unto him who does not desire or care for anything.
- Be content with whatever you do, without attachment or sense of ownership.
- He is a brave man who can say 'no'. Desire is increased by desire.
- When we feel and accept God's will at all times, how can we want anything?
- I possess nothing, therefore I renounce nothing - I want nothing, as I am everything.
- Neither seek nor avoid, take what comes; this is contentment.
- When you accept life, life accepts you. Allow your nature to carry out the will of higher power.
- You cannot buy bliss with money.

- One who possesses is possessed; one who is contented is liberated.
- Love bestows upon the receiver but gives to the giver too. Be not miserly in love.
- Love knows no bargaining, asks nothing but gives everything in which individuality vanishes and there is communion.
- If you decide to love a person even with his faults, then it is not chance, it's your choice.
- We waste time looking for the perfect lover, instead of creating the perfect love.
- Love is not an action but a state of mind.
- Love is the Master Key to open door of liberation.
- Love is the saviour of Life; it bestows supreme peace and everlasting joy.
- Have an encouraging, positive, cheerful, hopeful and loving attitude.
- It is good to forgive but best is to forget.
- Man is ever in debt for the welfare given to him and therefore can have no claim or demand on anyone.
- Our life is what our thoughts make it.
- Man can work his own miracles, provided he has faith, conviction and equanimity.
- Fame is a communicable disease.
- Your goal is to discover infinity worth in yourself.
- Every situation in life will change. Favourable and unfavourable times will come and go. Therefore, do not seek God's blessing for objects.
- A true seeker never expects God to alter or change his situation as predicaments come according to one's own destiny and deeds.
- Have faith and Shradha in yourself. Ignite the light of wisdom within. Surrender yourself to God without any ego, cleverness or shrewdness.
- Don't try to change people, accept them as they are.
- If you are changed, the whole world is changed for you.

- Impartial justice is the greatest mercy of God.
- God gives what you need and not what you want or desire.
- Relinquish your need for external approval; you alone are the judge of your worth.
- Believe and trust in the Goodness and caring power of God. Thy 'will' be done.
- Count your blessing and be grateful to the Almighty.
- Confession is a virtue of few.
- When you are in anger or opposition with circumstances, realise that you are struggling within yourself.
- When you relinquish your anger, you will be healing yourself and cooperating with the flow of the Universe.
- I want to be happy; but I can be happy only if I make others happy.
- Devotion to God increases in the same proportion as attachment to the objects of the senses decreases.
- Keep yourself busy; you will have no time for worrying.
- Be clean, not clever. See no evil in others.
- The world is like water and the mind of a man like milk. Milk will mix with water if you put the two together. But turn the milk into curd, then churn it and have butter. Now, if you keep the butter in water it will not mix with the water but float unattached. So keep your heart and mind unattached with the materialistic world.
- Life is a challenge   -   Meet it.
- Life is a gift   -   Accept it.
- Life is a sorrow   -   Overcome it
- Life is a duty   -   Perform it.
- Life is a game   -   Play it.
- Life is a song   -   Sing it.
- Life is a promise   -   Fulfil it.
- Life is love   -   Enjoy it.
- Life is smile   -   Give it to others.
- Life is an experience   -   Share it with others.

- Life is knowledge   -   Distribute it.
- Life is a charity   -   Donate it.

The most fortunate happening of my existence is that I have been born as a 'Human Being' with superior faculties, to ensure that the human body so awarded, is properly maintained.

We spend one-third of our lives sleeping and the rest of our life earning. Out of that, half of our lives we waste in ruining our health and the other half in taking care of it. Apart from healthy thoughts, dieting and exercise should have due priority in our daily agenda.

EATING HABITS

It is healthy to remember that diet should be what our body needs and not what our tongue desires. We should eat nutritive food with more fruits and vegetables as per the requirement of our body. A regular meal pattern has to be established with fairly consistent 'times' for each meal. Since there is a longer time gap and rest during night, it is said that one should eat like a prince at breakfast, a king at lunch and a pauper at dinner.

Moderation in eating: Deliver yourself from the temptation of succumbing to your palate or eating more than is adequate for the body. Eat within the limits of your hunger. While slightly lesser intake is a good habit, overeating is always harmful. Learn to freeze the 'Moments' you find yourself tempted to fall a victim to taste or to overeat. Be an observer, which gives you a chance to control and recover yourself from indulgence. We have to realise that we eat to live and not live to eat.

YOGA

Yoga keeps you fit, increases your life-span and reduces stress. Exercise also improves your stamina and sharpens your reflexes. It is amazing to hear the number of excuses one can find to be lethargic, e.g. 'where is the time?', 'I am good enough!', 'I am too old for this'. We should not deny ourselves the benefits of getting up early before sunrise and deriving pleasures like breathing in the fresh morning air, enjoying the peaceful 'silence' of the occasion when we really become one with 'nature'.

We need a warm-up, stretch and cool-down pattern of exercise of say 30 minutes duration. It could be in the form of spot-jogging, skipping, cycling, swimming, walking, running or out-door sports.

Yoga is one of the most sublime forms of exercise. It is of great benefit with focus on spiritual, mental and physical discipline. Under proper guidance, Yoga is very rejuvenating; combining breathing 'Pranayam' and 'Asanas' exercises. The regimen could be tailored to suit individual requirements.

This has been discussed and explained in detail in the chapter: 'Adopting the Vedic Culture' of this book.

–3–
The Role of Vedic Culture to Enjoy Beneficial Living

Vedic Philosophy

The aim of Vedic Philosophy is to first discover the secret laws of the Universe and then evolve a pattern to be used for everyday life from those laws.

I have attempted to take a microscopic section from the magnificent Vedic Period to discover the scientific reasons to show how close the people are to nature, and, thereby, learn the art of meaningful and beneficial living.

To derive the desired benefit in true spirit, let us clearly distinguish the known from the unknown.

The Mystery of the Unknown is the essence of all activities of human achievements. The Unknown truth is always a concept, it can only be realised by the Soul, it cannot be materialised, because it vanishes the moment you reach that point. Every 'CREATION' emerges from the Unknown that was there from the beginning of all beginnings.

Shloka

> AUM Purnamadah Purnamidam Purnat Purnam Udachyate
> Purnasya Purnmadaya Purnameva Vashishyate

Meaning:- This is perfect, that is perfect; from the perfect the perfect emerges. If perfect is deducted from perfect only the perfect remains.

The Vedantic learning process insists on constantly reminding us of the following principles in the form of peace invocation chanted before starting every lesson.

SHLOKA

> Sehnavavtu Sehnobhunaktu Sehviryam Keravavahai,
> Tejasvina Wadhitamastu Ma Vidvishavahai
> AUM Shanti Shanti Shanti

MEANING

> Let Him protect us both,
> We be blessed with the bliss of knowledge,
> Let us do the brave act together
> May our studies be thorough and faithful,
> May we never misunderstand each other,
> Oh Eternity, Peace, Peace, Peace.

To get perfect results it is always important to put a correct question than to give a correct answer to the wrong question.

THE RUDIMENTS OF VEDANTIC THOUGHTS

Nature has always been kind to mankind. If approached in true harmony, nature's innermost secrets can be revealed and their energies harnessed for the benefit of all living beings. Nature, Man and Product are all within the evolutionary network guided by our Karmas.

Vastu Shastra:- A Vedic architectural beauty is to be seen, felt, perceived, conceived and experienced.

While the present western generation is looking to the materialistic world for desired peace of mind and happiness, an open secret is relatively unknown that India is the fountainhead of the vast ancient Vedic knowledge that is the source of everlasting peace, bliss and joy.

When the Vedic concept is presented through modern technological advances, this sublime information becomes available and can be easily understood and applied to modern living.

In the Vedic period, people built homes and hermitages with a view to having a peaceful life, offer prayers and to live in Universal harmony.

However, in the modern world, people built concrete clusters of buildings, mainly for a high rate of return that has resulted in worldwide pollution, environmental and ecological problems and loss of peace of mind.

The Vedic concept was derived with a view to helping mankind live in peace, harmony and happiness on this planet.

SHLOKA

> Sarve Bhavantu Sukhinah Sarve Santu Niramaya,
> Sarve Bhadrani Pashyantu Ma Kaschid dukhbhagbhavet.

Meaning

> May all be happy. May all be free from disabilities, May all look to the good of others, May none suffer from sorrow. Let the whole world be in peace and prosperity.

One ponders to find answers to vital questions like:-

- How did the Universe evolve?
- What is the real constitution of a human being?
- What is the Ultimate?

The Vedas proclaim that the divine consciousness is without beginning or end, it is Omnipresent, Omnipotent and Omniscient.

The 'Eternal' contains:
- Space (Akash)
- Time (Kaal)
- Energy (Prana)
- Nature (Prakriti)

This all-pervading consciousness regulates the entire Cosmos and gives a spark of life to all individual beings.

The distinction between the eternal spirit, the soul and the changing material body:

As the embodied soul continually passes into material body from childhood to youth to old age, the soul similarly passes into the astral body after death. The material body merges with the five elements of nature.

THE VEDAS SAY

- There are laws of creation.
- The law of maintenance and evolution.
- The law of dissolution.

The rudiments of Vedantic thoughts can be depicted in Trimurti.

Brahma - The Creator
Vishnu - The Sustainer
Mahesh - The Annihilator

Innumerable laws that are always in a state of evolution govern the Universe.

THE MAN is the only creature that is blessed with the power of mind, which is the unique creation of the great designer.

To enjoy this grand play of consciousness, the Leela of Purusha and Prakriti, one has to:

- Observe it
- Discover it
- Enjoy it
- Create out of it and merge into it again

The Three-Letter Mahamantra – 'AUM' – The symbol of the divinity that pervades the Universe.

The first sound vibration of the Universe was 'AUM'.

The Mahamantra 'AUM' represents the eternal endlessness of the Universe (time and space) and, therefore, endlessness of knowledge and information.

'AUM' is the healing mantra predicting:

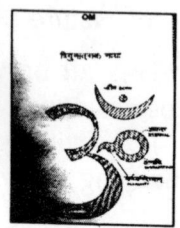

Diag. 1

- Satt (Truth)
- Chit (Mind)
- Anand (Happiness)

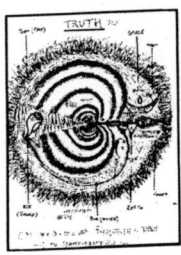

Diag. 2

In regular meditation and Japa, "AUM" produces such an enormous and powerful vibration that it virtually gives emergence to the five elements (Space, Air, Fire, Water and Earth) of which, the entire Srishti - the Universe is composed of.

WHAT ARE THE VEDAS?

The Vedas are a systematic and formulated source of knowledge that explain the relationship between Man, Nature and God.

The Vedas train us to think and rediscover ourselves, analyse, investigate and realise the very essence of life. Living a contented life is an art, a skill, a technique which all of us need to learn and master to achieve mental peace and harmony.

The Vedas help us in creating and maintaining a proper balance between body, mind, intellect and the five elements of nature. They help us in reducing the stress and strain of materialistic life, leading to a state of ultimate liberation and bliss.

The Vedas offer us a practical way of life that satisfies our spiritual need and gives Mental Peace along with material prosperity.

Your very self is an ocean with a fortune of undiscovered wealth deep inside you and the unbounded love that you can offer to others. Your mind is so powerful that you can create an environment of your own choice around you.

Let us all be true seekers and devote ourselves to reach the state of ultimate Bliss and liberation.

The Science and Philosophy of the Vedas is the answer to all the needs of mankind.

In order to seek the scientific answers to all questions and to understand the role of Vedic culture in our modern day to day living, our Rishis and Munis, who had a deep knowledge of the laws of nature, developed a number of scientific systems which are explained in the Vedas.

Some of them are given below:-

- Vastu Shastra
  Vastu Kala, Vastu Manav Shilpa, Vastu Shilpa Shastra, Vastu Deva Shilpa, Vastu Science and the Five elements of Nature.
- Health and Spirituality
- Meditation and Yoga
- Ayurveda, Vedic, Herbal, Divine and Spiritual Plants
- Mantra, Yantra, Prayer and Spiritual Healing
- Vedic Systems for a healthy body, mind, soul and environment

SHLOKA

"Na pranena na apranena martyo jivati Kaschana,
Itarena tu jivanti yasmin etavapasritau."

Meaning:- Our life does not depend merely on the breathing process or the intake of food, which are no doubt, important for the body, but health does not survive on food alone. Everything can be thrown out of order if the mind is upset.

A turbulence injected into the mind is enough to disturb the entire balance of personality.

Our Consciousness comprises of three stages of awareness:

- Waking
- Dreaming
- Deep sleep

We also have three behavioural qualities:

'Satvic', 'Rajasic' and 'Tamasic': Spiritual, psychological or merely lethargic ways of living. We are taught that by knowledge, selfless service and meditation we can achieve the ultimate.

- Knowledge can be derived from **'Yantras'**
- Creativity from **'Tantras'**
- Energies from **'Mantras'**
- Inspiration from **'Meditation'**

I have combined all these together in my practice of Vastu to achieve best results. This would give a new outlook to the world of Vedic architecture, based on Vastu Shastra and Vedic Culture.

THE TOTAL MAN

If Man is the reflection of Nature, Vedas reflect Man and his total personality. Human body and mind are complex instruments which communicate, absorb, expand and get consumed by nature. (Man, Vedas and Nature are the natural evolutionary extensions of one another, forming a complete whole.)

OUR ATTITUDE TOWARDS THE VEDAS

These days, the entire world is seriously concerned about the ecological imbalance, environment and pollution. However, our ancient Rishis and Munis have given us these mantras thousands of years ago.

Shanti Path:

> The Vedas Say:- AUM Dyau Shanti Antariksh gvam, Shanti Prithvi, Shanti Rapah, Shanti Roshadhaya, Shanti Vanaspatya, Shanti Vishvedevah, Shanti Brahma, Shanti Servagyum, Shanti Shanti Revah, Shanti Sa Ma, Shanti Redhi, AUM Shanti Shanti Shanti AUM ll

The peace that resides in the environment, in the Solar World, in Space, in the Earth and Elementary Water, nourishes the herbs, fruits and grains thereby nourishing the original power in all beings. May the peace of the world now and forever come into us, we pray, May the highest good prevail.

Cosmic energy from Sun, Air, Light and Colour balances man, material and nature for sustaining health and happiness to enjoy beneficial living.

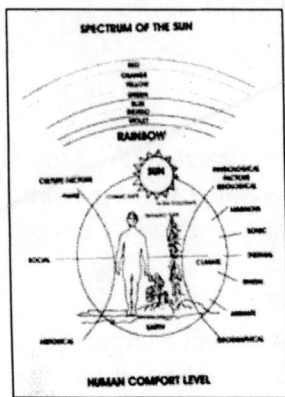

Diag. 3

Exposure to Sunlight

The Human body, is truly a living photocell which is energised by Sunlight.

Sunlight and fresh air are the basic elements from which all life originates, develops, heals and evolves. Light and Air play a vital role in the formation of principles of Vastu Shastra.

Shloka

>Dhaunch ma Idam Prithvi Chantariksh cha me Vyachaha
>Agnihi Surya aapo Medham Vishve Devascha Sam Dadhu

(Atharva Ved 12/1/53)

Meaning

>Heaven, Sun, Earth and fresh Air
>Have given me this wide space,
>And all Cosmic Powers
>Together have endowed me with Intellect

(Atharva Ved 12/1/53)

Benefits of exposure to morning sunlight:

- Produces Vitamin D in the body resulting in normal growth and development of bones
- Decreases Blood Sugar
- Balances Blood Pressure
- Decreases resting heart rate
- Decreases respiratory rate
- Decreases Lactic Acid in blood
- Increases resistance to Arthritis

ULTRAVIOLET LIGHT is an effective treatment for many

diseases. Sun therapy is very commonly used in Naturopathy and is included in treatment of anemia, gout, colitis, cystitis, arthritis, eczema, acne, herpes, lupus, sciatica, asthma, kidney problems and even burns.

Scientific Evidence:

- *UV Light increases the efficiency of the heart:* At the Tulane School of Medicine, Dr. Raymond Johnson exposed 20 people to Ultraviolet Light. In 18 out of 20 people, their cardiac output increased an average of 39%! In other words, their hearts became stronger and pumped more blood.
- *UV Light is an effective treatment for Psoriasis:* Reports from the National Psoriasis Foundation indicate that 80% of those suffering from this skin disease improve when they are exposed to UV Light.
- *UV Light activates the synthesis of Vitamin D:* Dr. Robert Neer and his Associate Scientists conducted a study on a group of elderly persons to determine if extra sunlight would increase their ability to absorb calcium from their diets. The group which did not receive UV rays had 25% decrease in Calcium absorption while the other group receiving UV Rays had a 15% increase in absorption.
- *UV Light increases the level of sex hormones:* In a study at Boston State Hospital, Dr. Abraham Myerson found that Ultraviolet light increased male hormone levels by 120% and activate Malatonin, a skin hormone.
- *UV Light is an effective treatment for many diseases:* It is also found very effective in killing infectious bacteria, including AFB which causes tuberculosis.

In 1903, Dr. Niels Finsen of Denmark was awarded the Nobel Prize for being the first person to successfully treat skin tuberculosis with Ultraviolet Light.

It is very important to know and study in depth, the UV Light and Infrared Rays, but we must also know that too much

UV light is bad, "we need a basic amount to support life and maintain a healthy immune system."

Rhythm of Life From Sunrise to Sunset

From Sunrise to Sunset, the environment and colour changes correspondingly affect all living things. The very first sunrise to sunset, we continue to be blessed by the beauty, power, life creating and life sustaining properties emanating from light. This is one of the important principles of Vastu Shastra.

Yoga and Meditation

- Increases energy and strength in the body
- Increases tolerance to stress
- Balances the breathing rhythm
- Increases ability of blood to absorb and carry oxygen
- Increases storage of oxygen

The Cosmic Cycle

The Cosmic Cycles affect our universe, which in turn affects the Solar System, which further affects the Earth and its climate, seasons and inhabitants, right down to the smallest particle within an atom. This is what Vastu Shastra explains.

What the Vedas Say

Most of the present generation spends its working hours indoors eliminating the morning sunlight and fresh air from their daily needs. It is therefore, very necessary to discuss and discover the indoor environment particularly in the 21st century, where the environment throughout the world is becoming more and more polluted, in relation to our health, productivity, universal peace and general well being.

Shloka

Shastrenanena Sarvasaya Lokasya Param Sukham I
Chaturvarga Phalaprapti Shlokashch Bhavedyuvam II
Shilpshastra Parigyan Mrityoapi Sujetam Vrajet I

Parmanand Janak Devanamidamiritam ||
Shilp Vina Nahi Jagtishu Lokeshu Vidyate |
Jagad Vina Na Shilpanch Vertate Vasav Prabho ||

Vastu Science provides good health, happiness and all-round prosperity to the entire Universe. Human beings attain divinity with this knowledge. Followers of Vastu Shastra not only get worldly pleasures but also experience heavenly bliss.

In this regard, Vedic Culture and Vastu Shastra play a very important role to help in building a clean environment, free from pollution of any kind, full of light and colour needed for the development of a healthy NATION with a peaceful environment by balancing Man, Material and Nature within the framework of the Five Elements of Nature.

Here I would like to give a few important tips, especially to Medical Practitioners to adopt in Hospitals and Nursing Homes for the speedy recovery of their patients.

The Vastu Research Centre, New Delhi conducted a study in which the following Vastu Principles were applied to different patients.

The results of the study revealed that 70% to 85% patients showed remarkable progress and their recovery rate was from 30% to 45% faster than the other patients.

1. *Orientation of Patient Room:*

- The patient room should have plenty of natural daylight with cross-ventilation, soft décor, fresh flowers, green plants and pleasant paintings or photographs on the walls
- Have maximum openings (windows) on the N/E, East or S/E walls
- No mirrors should be kept in the room
- Use only **wooden beds** and avoid steel or metal frame beds.

2. *Colour Scheme:*

The ceiling and three walls of the room must be off-white and the wall towards the West should be light green in colour. Do not use any synthetic paints.

3. *Electrical Wiring:*

All electrical wiring should be in conduit pipes with both ends properly earthed. Do not use fluorescent tube lights. Use only bulbs. Avoid the use of electric blanket or electric mattress.

4. *Air Conditioning:*

Use only window A/Cs with fresh air vents in the "open" position. If using a Central air conditioning with duct system, add minimum 15% to 20% fresh air.

5. *Entertainment:*

No Television. Only pleasant soothing music or Bhajans to be played at fixed times. Play soft instrumental music or some healing Mantras and Prayer for different patients in consultation with the Vastu Consultant.

It was proven with evidence that patients who were given "distance prayer healing" recovered at a rate that was more than 18% faster than other patients.

6. *Sleeping position:*

- Generally, in normal conditions, the patient's head should be towards the East.
- If there is excessive bleeding after the operation keep the head towards the North but only for a few days.
- For patients suffering from Asthma or breathing problems, the head should be towards the North-West.
- For patients suffering from Low Blood Pressure, Anaemia or Heart problems, their heads should be towards the South.
- Never keep the bed below a hanging beam.
- Pregnant ladies' heads should be towards the west. Never keep the head towards the North or South.
- After delivery, the head should be towards the East.

- During the delivery, the overhead light in the OT Room should be switched off. Use normal indirect light.
- Never bring the new-born baby into bright light.
- Keep the baby in a room with pink walls, good eastern light and cross ventilation.

Towards the 21st Century

FOGGING THE ATMOSPHERE

Unless preventive measures are taken, by the year 2008, moving, living and even breathing will be a problem in big cities with generator sets and vehicular pollution accounting for 75 % of the air, noise and smoke pollution. Fogging the atmosphere further are the thermal power plants that contribute 13% and assorted industrial activity adds another 12%.

With the number of vehicles being added daily on the roads, the number of people injured or killed in road accidents during 2002 is about 45% higher than the figure for the corresponding period in 1990.

Plastic and Solid Waste Management plans are just not in place. The present consumption patterns indicate that garbage volumes will more than double by the year 2008. This will leave 40% of the total garbage scattered all over with no viable collection or recycling plan.

It is estimated that the total average energy consumed by man in the past 2000 years, has been consumed in the last half century only.

SPEED OF HUMAN MOVEMENT

In olden days, the fastest transportation available to man for long distance travel was up to a maximum of twenty miles per hour.

Today, men in space capsules are circling the earth at approximately 30,000 kilometres per hour.

DEVELOPMENT

The overwhelming majority of advanced technology and electronic gadgets like TV, Computer, Cell phone, Microwave

Oven, etc that we use in our daily life today have been developed only within the present lifetime.

What is evident from all the above examples is the fact that we are developing at an accelerated rate which itself is accelerating and leaving our own rich culture far behind.

However, the acceleration of change is going to deeply penetrate our private lives and will place absolutely unprecedented strains on the family. By 2005, an average adult may have to face eight times more stress.

Family of the future?

Career and status consciousness in the fair sex has made life more mechanical and the quality time one spent with his family has decreased still further. Now the possibilities are threefold:

1. Family life will be dead except for the first few years of child-raising.
2. The family is for a Golden Age:
   With advances in Information Technology, homes and offices will become coincident. People may not have to move out of their homes because they would be able to do most of their jobs and shopping from their homes on E-mail, Web Site or on the Internet. As free time and leisure increase, the families will spend more time together and will derive greater satisfaction from joint activity.
3. The future is more open than it might appear. The family may either vanish or entering a new Golden Age, it may break up and shatter only to come together again in weird and novel ways like contract marriages.

Let us discuss some possibilities that may altogether revolutionise the concept of family as compared to the Vedic Age.

Concept of Motherhood?

Advanced Birth technology is going to have the most upsetting effect on the family.

The extension of the test tube baby concept may lead to babies which can be grown in a laboratory jar - what happens to the notion of maternity then? And what happens to the self image of the female in societies.

BIRTH OF THE SUPER HUMAN?

Skin grafting techniques are commonly employed these days in plastic surgery and allied fields. In fact, if the top R and D people of surgery are to be believed, very shortly human limbs can be developed in labs.

It might be possible to develop the human brain in laboratories within the next 25 to 50 years. Brain transplants can come even sooner.

Lord Shiva had transplanted an elephant head to the human body.

Ancient Egyptians used to keep their dead bodies inside a pyramid properly preserved in the hope that some day it might be possible to inject life back into them.

The present Medical Researchers are actively involved in research in which, they probably think that it would now be possible to do so.

All of these are likely to cause great social stresses. In fact, the final question that arises is:

If life and death can also be governed by human beings, what happens to our concept of God? And who, in that case, will control all these super humans with super brains or the technocrats?

Finally, who is going to decide which individual is to be converted into a superhuman?

Will the concepts of "crime and punishment" change? Will the concept of "power and ego" hazards vanish?

Will life become so mechanical that everyone does a set of jobs that have been pre-programmed in his mind?

If life becomes so mechanical, then what right will we have to call ourselves human beings – will we not be reduced to being machines?

All these possibilities need to be given further thought so that we are prepared to face them whenever they crop up.

The answer lies with the Vedas and in the Vedic knowledge.

CONCLUSION

- The human race in the 21st century is encountering changes at a tremendous speed. A number of opportunities as well as challenges are lying in the lap of the future and unless we gear up to face those challenges—to grab those opportunities within a proper time frame—we are in for a massive adaptation breakdown.
- The social stresses which will be generated by the developmental forces might lead to the total collapse of human civilisation and we will be doomed if we do not prepare for them accordingly.
- On the contrary, proper channelisation of these forces and suitable adjustment in our values will make life much more easier, much more comfortable; a life really worth living, but one must know the art of living with the help of Vedic Knowledge and to apply Vastu Shastra in our Modern Living with full knowledge and understanding.
- Your strength is within you. Religion begins where science ends and marks the beginning of the higher wisdom.

THE UNIVERSAL PRAYER

Aum asaoto maa sadgamaya
Tamaso maa jyotirgamaya
Mruytorma amrutam gamaya
Aum Shantih ! Shantih !! Shantih !!!

Meaning:- O Lord, lead me from the unreal to the ultimate reality, from darkness to light, and from the death of ignorance to the immortality of knowledge.

–4–
The Five Elements and Their Scientific Application for Blissful Living

Sages and saints who wrote down the texts on the subject had kept in mind the influence of the sun; the soul of this Universe, the moon, the effect of other planets and their light and heat on the earth and its living beings, the earth's atmosphere, wind, its directions, earth's magnetic field, gravitational forces, Electromagnetic field and various planets like Moon, Jupiter, Mars and other natural factors.

Human beings have also created unwanted, unnatural waves and rays against nature like radio active material, telecommunication and other audio and video waves, photocells, X-Rays, cellular phones, infrared rays, other sound waves to name just a few.

The human mind is the subject, object and cause of Vastu. It perceives and conceives Vastu in relation to experiences of itself with the surrounding world and its influence.

Man as a tool making animal, designs and controls his environment. The environmental changes created by him to suit his choices of living and working directly reflects his personal, social, material, emotional, intellectual and vital personalities.

Through the act of design, he alters and moulds the elements of the natural environment. The sequences of the natural elements used as 'The Mediums' or 'The Materials' are as follows:

Earth, Water, Air, Sun and Space.

Earth and Water have limited and localised availability for human habitat and growth. Since the earth and water have cognisable physical bodies, they are the apparent and fundamental choice makers in the location and the physical form of the Vedic architecture and habitat.

Though the sun, air and space also form select priorities for comfortable human life, these are apparently universally available and can be moulded to human need by the act of design by earth and water. Among all these, water is a shy element. Habitat, therefore, goes where water is. Only in some very special situations, water is diverted to the site of the habitat. However, this decision is often expensive and not feasible, economically as well as ecologically.

Ideal / habitats, cultures, Vastu and life have naturally shown exhilarence where all the five physical elements to support life are abundantly available and are suitable to human growth and evolution.

The oldest, the rich and the living civilisations all over the globe have been along the temperate zones *i.e.* the zone of Cancer and the zone of Capricorn where the evolution of the human mind reached its peak at the earliest.

The records of present history go back by almost 5000 years, when one knows that about 4000 years ago, in these regions, the human super minds lived. In other regions such as the Equator or the colder regions, civilisations and cultures developed much later.

In order to understand the act of design with these five physical elements, we shall take each one separately to appreciate their meaning, role and applicability in Vastu. Broadly, for the present, they form their scope for human habitat as follows:

Earth

Land structure, landform, landscape, flora and fauna. It also establishes availability of local construction materials and their work ability, eco-friendly raw building material. It provides us food, vegetables, fruits, mineral, medicinal and spiritual herbs.

Water

The habitat and physical life is where water is. This is true for all life forms and eco-cultures. The type, form and pattern of life also greatly depend on the relationship of the earth and water. The sea front, riverfront, lakefront, the underground water level or streams for wells are also important for flora to grow. Water is not the only life source, but it is unarguably, fundamental to location and growth of habitats.

Air

As a life-supporting element, air is a very powerful life source. Two minutes of blockage of air supply to the respiratory system can destroy life. Pure air with oxygen is good for the brain and the blood. Human physical comfort values are directly and sensitively dependent on the correct level of humidity, airflow, atmospheric temperature, air pressure, air composition and its contents. In this respect, air deals with the entire body surface through the skin, the respiratory and blood systems by way of respiration.

Building systems to handle air for comfort conditions have a direct impact on the form and visual qualities in buildings and habitats. Air also represents movement. Circulation of fresh air and cross ventilation in buildings is vital for a healthy house.

Sun

The Sun is a major source of energy. More than 90% of the Earth's energy comes from the Sun. The hot sun has a glare, sharp light and dark shadows. The cool sun has colours and it rarely rises above the horizon, or, often couples geographically with heavy clouds in the sky and snow on earth. The cool sun is generally gloomy but is beautiful to behold, silvery and with long hours of twilight.

Hot humid zones with heavy cloudy sky for longer periods of the year also have a distinctive culture in Vastu Shastra. The Sun has played an important role in the development of visual qualities of Vastu in terms of textures, colours, roof forms, and above all, expressions of vitality.

Space

All the above elements are skillfully engineered towards the creation of physically comfortable, emotionally pleasant, intellectually determinant, totally vibrant and blissfully satisfying spaces for human shelter and habitat. Man lives in space.

The main rule in Vastu Shastra for planning is, Orientation. Balancing the energy in relationship with human comfort level

From Space

1. Basic Elements	Sound
2. Technological aspects	Vibration
3. Instrument of Perception (a) To acquire Inward (b) To acquire Outward	 Ear Speech
4. Work Organs	Communication
5. Controlling Central Force Flow of Thoughts, Emotions or Joy	Mind
6. Presiding force	Cosmos Rays
7. Supreme Energy	Soul (Prana)

Vastu Architecture in Transformation Related to Material and Technology of SPACE

    (a) Silence
    (b) Acoustics
    (c) Reflection
    (d) Vibration
    (e) Texture Surface
    (f) Design Language System
    (g) Non-Measurable Dimensions Depicting Mental Comfort

To balance the energy relationship with human comfort level

From Air

1. Basic Elements	Touch
2. Technological Field	Climate
3. Instrument of Perception (a) To acquire Inward (b) To acquire Outward	Skin Finger
4. Work Organs	Hands
5. Controlling Central Force	Weather Conditioning
6. Presiding force	Circulation System

Vastu Architecture in Transformation Related to Material and Technology of AIR
   (A) Climatology: To study and apply in design
To balance the energy in relationship with human comfort level

From Fire

1. Basic Elements	Sun
2. Technological Field	Light
3. Instrument of Perception (a) To acquire Inward (b) To acquire Outward	Eyes Heat
4. Work Organs	Light and Heat
5. Controlling Central Force	Colour
6. Presiding force	Texture (Visual)

Vastu Architecture in Transformation Related to Material and Technology of FIRE
   (a) Light
   (b) Colour
   (c) Solar System Gain or Loss
To balance the energy in relationship with human comfort level

From Water

1.	Basic Elements	Taste
2.	Technological Field	Cooling
3.	Instrument of Perception (a) To acquire Inward (b) To acquire Outward	 Tongue Sweating
4.	Work Organs	Anus (Lower Part of the canal)
5.	Controlling Central Force	River
6.	Presiding force	Sea

Vastu Architecture in Transformation Related to Material and Technology of WATER
   (a) Plumbing
   (b) Heating and Cooling
   (c) Sewerage System
   (d) Drainage System
   (e) Water Management
   (f) Water Engineering
   (g) Flora, Water Fall, Fountain, Pool
   (h) Water Supply System Network and Disposal
To balance the energy in relationship with human comfort level

From Earth

1.	Basic Elements	Smell
2.	Technological Field	Basic Raw Material
3.	Instrument of Perception (a) To acquire Inward (b) To acquire Outward	 Nose Nose
4.	Work Organs	Genital Procreates
5.	Controlling Central Force	Formation
6.	Presiding force	Mud (Earth)

Vastu Architecture in Transformation Related to Material and Technology of EARTH
   (a) Basic Building Raw Material
   (b) Mud Architecture is famous internationally
   (c) Landscape
   (d) Insulation
   (e) Recycling

The Five Elements are Universal. The Science of Vastu is a complete building industry with ultra modern technology of building good relations between Man, Material and Nature, balancing the five elements, with an in-depth study of Micro-Weather at site with Climatical study.

From the above table one can clearly see:

A: How the various aspects of the physical body, senses, mind and their related manifestation in humanities, science and technology become interactive, relative, overlapping and integrated.

B: It also shows how the sciences of dimensioning emerge from the process.

One must realise at the outset that the language of Vastu is unique.

The following points must be kept in mind at all times:

1. It is very essential to learn to think, perceive, conceive, experience, act and produce, all simultaneously. Vastu Shastra is not a linear process. All linear tools of expression such as speech writing etc. fail to express this simultaneity. One should be able to think, observe, analyse, sketch, design, all in the simultaneous-led process in practice.

2. Man, his surroundings and methods are integral to each other. They form a kind of universe within a universal system. Any design action in Vastu is, therefore, relative and requires Holistic, Meditative and Creative processes.

Similarly, Nature, Man and Product are juxtapositioned within an evolutionary network. The Design processes in this network are guided by performance standards that are, again within the holistic framework, and therefore, relative to a given situation.

Vedic religion was thus the moving spirit of the organisation of Aryan Village communities. Indian lore is full of laws laid down in crystallised form by saints and scholars in every branch of learning. The process by which such universal laws were arrived at may be unknown to us. Most of the cases are found perfect and are applicable even today. Nothing was left undirected. The execution of even the minutest detail had laws governing it.

The principles laid down in Vastu Shastra for the construction of dwellings, even today, seem amazingly scientific. The religious mystery given to the whole process gave birth to superstitions that generally arise from exaggerating a logical reasoning. The religious connotations were probably employed to keep the law makers (kings), and brahmins (priests) from being transparent. Rituals gave the whole process a sacred dimension, which ensured that every little detail was efficiently carried out.

The **MIND** is the author and the Lord of man's physical world around him.

The Vastu Shastra learning process insists on reminding us constantly of the following principles in the form of invocations chanted for peace before starting every lesson. Chanting deals with the holistic attitude and with the need to constantly work together in a team.

These are reproduced here in the English transcript and translation.

SHLOKA

> Purnamadah Purnamidam Purnat Purnnam Udachayate,
> Purnasya Purnmadaya Purnmeve Vashishyate,
> *OM, SHANTI, SHANTI, SHANTI !*

MEANING

This is perfect, that is perfect and from the perfect, the perfect emerges. If perfect is deducted from the perfect, only the perfect remains. Oh! Eternity Peace, Peace, Peace!

The Five Elements—Blissful Living

Shloka

Sahanavavtu Sehnobhunaktu,
Sahveeryam Karavavahi,
Tejasvinavadhi Tamastu, Maha Vidvishavahi
OM, SHANTI, SHANTI, SHANTI !

Meaning

Let Him protect us both. Be blessed with the bliss of knowledge. Let us do the brave act together. May our studies be thorough and faithful. May we not misunderstand each other. Oh! Eternity Peace, Peace, Peace!

The last two lines are a warning towards the possible lack of accuracy and thoroughness of 'the Generalist'. It also highlights that lack of communication results in misunderstanding or misapplication of information or knowledge to design. Thorough understanding, right application and meaningful communication are important to team work.

The Total Man

According to the Upanishads, an average human being possesses five senses while the super human intellectual man can open his sixth sense, called **'The Third Eye of Cosmic Vision'**.

The Perfect Man consists of 16 Kalas, 3 states of awareness and 3 states of behavioural qualities as follows:

The Kalas:
1. Prana
2. Faith
3. Akasha
4. Air
5. Fire
6. Water
7. Earth
8. The Senses
9. Mind
10. Food
11. Strength

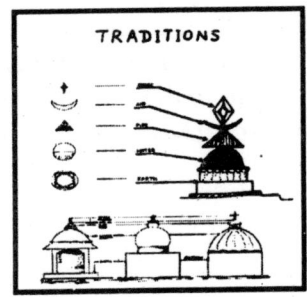

12. Thought
13. Mantra
14. Karma
15. The World
16. Names

The three states of awareness are:
- Awake
- Dream
- Sleep

The three behavioural states are:
- Tamas
- Rajas
- Satva

Let us now understand and study the transfer process between Nature, Man and Vastu. If man is reflection of Nature, Vastu reflects man and his total personality. The human body and mind are complex instruments that communicate, absorb, expand and get consumed by nature. Nature, Man and Vastu are the natural evolutionary extensions of one another, forming a complete whole.

The five elements of this planet are Earth, Water, Fire, Air and Space as explained in the Vastu Graphic Symbols.

There is a flame that burns within all of us. It is what we call the spirit (the soul). To keep this flame burning and illuminate our lives, one must always be truthful to one's inner self.

The Universal Truth is embodied in various forms within us. It is up to the individual to keep it alive. Very often, the fear of failure, fear of non-acceptance, fear of losing etc. holds us back. One must break free of all barriers and dare to be oneself. In the final analysis, it is only those people who love and accept you for how you are, that matters.

–5–
The Mind

THE MYSTERY OF "THE UNKNOWN"

The Unknown is the essence of all activities of the human mind. The horizon is always a concept, because it vanishes the moment you reach that point. The Horizon has its reality in 'IMAGINATION' or 'CREATIVITY'. It emerges from the beginning of all the beginnings.

Every time one goes deep into the SOURCE and looks for the IMPULSE, or RATIONALE, a process, a method follows. Life sprouts in impulses.

THE MIND

The mind is the Lord and author of man's physical world around and within him.

The mind mainly operates at two levels:

1. The external (convex) mind receives and reflects all information from the Prakriti (the external world of names and forms). The physical world consists of five elements; Space, Air, Water, Fire and Earth. These represent Sound, Touch, Taste, Sight and Smell. They are the sensory organs for communication with the physical world. Thus, the mind may be fed information as per the 'interests' or conditioning of the sensory organs. The objectives of the sensory organs are Artha, Kama and Dharma (Wealth, Comfort and Glory). The external surface of the mind is in constant touch with the external world and its nature to be constantly mobile, so as to efficiently perform its basic job to keep in touch with Prakriti and to transmit the information.

This wandering mind is constantly in a state of demand, desires, feelings of incompleteness. It is always wanting, never satisfied. This state of mind makes man feel insecure, weak and lacking in confidence. Man, therefore, looks for psychological and moral support all the time viz. support for any MEDIUM (religion, guru, work, people, drugs, friends, company, society, medical, physical, moral or knowledge).

2. The function of the core mind or the inner mind is to communicate with Purusha. However, unlike the Outer Mind, it does not depend on external or physical sensory instruments. This mind trains itself to be self-operative. An untrained mind may realise the presence of this capacity at times; but it does not have the capacity to operate this facility at will.

Unlike Prakriti, Purusha is stable, timeless, ageless, continuous, pure consciousness, a source of creativity, the beginning of all beginnings, the life behind all Prakriti.

The inner mind is introverted, quiet and lapsed have a constant source of truth, solitude and happiness. It is made of Satvika aspects of the five elements and sheaths (physical, emotional, intellectual, vital energy and bliss). Its goal is to establish communication between Atman and Paramatman and merge it with when detached from the mind - body complex. This mind never dies and has continuity with time and space. The information collected, stored and processed by individual minds gets transmitted to the universal over a large geographical region.

The mind collects information mainly from the two sensory organs i.e. Eyes and Ears (what you see and what you hear).

The eyes can perform their function of seeing only when there is light within the eyes as well as outside in the environment. Only then can one see, visualise and marvel at the beauty of nature.

In darkness, when there is no light within or outside, what the eyes experience is only a sense of dark black colour.

The images seen by the eyes are stored in the mind, which in turn, processes the images and segregates them into good images and bad or unpleasant images. One likes to see the

The Mind

good images time and again; but would not like to see the bad images a second time.

Similarly, the ears pick up all the sound vibrations around us, be it soothing, pleasant sounds or unpleasant, jarring sounds. They may emanate from persons close to our hearts or from enemies. These sound vibrations are transmitted to the mind, which in turn analyses and edits the sound waves. Obviously, one would like to listen to the soothing and pleasant sounds and block the unpleasant or jarring sounds.

It is obvious from the above that the mind controls the organs of our body.

For example, you are physically present in a classroom and attentively listening to the teacher's lecture word by word. Suddenly, your mind loses its concentration and your thoughts go to a Beach Party that you had attended last month. You recall with pleasure, the fun you had with all your friends, the music, dancing, the delicious food and the spectacular view as the sun set over the ocean. You experience a lot of joy as you relive those great moments. Suddenly, your teacher jolts you out of your reverie and pulls you up for daydreaming. You say that your attention was very much in the class. The teacher then asks you to repeat what was being said in the class. Your mind is blank, as you were not paying any attention to the lecture. You were physically present in the class, but you were neither seeing the teacher nor listening to the lecture. However, your mind was miles away at the party!

The mind plays a very important role in your past, present and future. It works tirelessly night and day, nonstop 24 hours a day. Even while your body is resting or is fast asleep, the mind is continuously working; it is either dreaming or contemplating the What? Why? and How? of life.

If you feel that you are tired, then you are tired, if you think that you are old, you start feeling old; and if you are in the company of children, you feel young and energetic. Every human being likes to feel good, young, energetic and cheerful.

When we see an illiterate labourer toiling away on the roadside, we tend to think that he has to undergo these physical hardships because he either has no brain or whatever brain he has is very weak.

On the other hand, we think that a professionally qualified intellectual has a very big or sharp brain. If both the brains, that of the ignorant labourer and that of the intellectual, are analysed by any Neurologist, it would be found that the size, volume and the structure of the brain cells are almost identical in both the brains!

The obvious question then comes up is: If both brains are identical, then why is there such a big difference in the performance of the brains?

The answer to the question lies in the fact that there is a vast difference in the training of their respective 'MINDS'.

The labourer, due to adverse circumstances, is deprived of the opportunity to obtain the right kind of stimulus for his mind and, as a consequence, the development of his mind and his thinking capacity is stinted.

On the other hand, the minds of the intellectuals (the Engineers, Architects, Doctors, Scientists, Scholars, Lawyers, Pilots, etc) are provided the appropriate stimuli right from the time of their birth through the formative years of their life. These stimuli help in developing the mind and they become experts in their chosen fields.

Similarly, we can train our minds to feel good, cheerful, young and disciplined at all times.

Five ways to balance the mind:

1. Silence

Silence is very powerful. The Golden Rule is to speak less and listen more. God, while developing the prototypes of our bodies, decided to give us one mouth and two ears. Why? So that we speak less and listen more! We must make it a habit to maintain silence (Maaun) for a minimum of one hour everyday.

2. Meditation

Meditation everyday morning and in the evening helps in

controlling the mind and prevents it from wandering here and there. The human mind is similar to the hard disk of a computer. When it gets overloaded with data, we have to delete some items, which have lost their utility. Similarly, when the mind is overloaded with feelings, emotions and thoughts, meditation helps us in purging the unwanted and unpleasant portions of our feelings, emotions and thoughts. This refreshes the mind and we are then able to think and see in a much brighter perspective.

3. Non - Judgement

Do not judge any person or pass judgement unnecessarily in situations where it is unwarranted. Remember, when we point a finger at others, three fingers are pointed back at us!

4. Nature

Spend time regularly in direct communion with nature, it not only enables us to sense the harmonious interaction of all the elements of nature and forces of life, but also gives us a sense of unity and love with all of life and develops the feeling of endless rhythm. Whether it be a stream, a forest, a mountain, a lake, a garden, the seashore or beautiful flowers, the communion with nature will also help you access the field of pure potentiality.

5. Innermost Essence

We must learn to get in touch with the innermost essence of our being. This true essence is beyond the ego. It is fearless, it is free, it is immune to criticism, it does not fear any challenge, it is beneath no one, superior to no one, and full of magical mystery and enchantment.

Access to our essence will also give us insight into the mirror of relationship, because all relationships are a reflection of our own relationships with ourselves.

Just for example, if you have fear, guilt, or are feeling insecure financially or success, then these are reflections of fear, guilt or insecurity as basic aspects of your personality. No individual, or money or success will solve these basic problems of existence. Only intimacy with the self will bring about true healing.

When you really understand your true nature, you will never feel guilty or insecure, because you will realise that the essence of material wealth is life energy, it is pure potentiality, which is your intrinsic nature, your thought of mind.

As you gain more and more access to your true nature, you will also spontaneously receive creative thoughts with pure knowledge.

Always keep in mind that the five elements of nature and the beautiful things around you in the environment give positive energy, colour, heat, light, vegetable, trees, flowers etc. They exude positive energy very silently, without any ego.

For example, the Sun silently gives us light, colour, heat, Ultraviolet Rays and Vitamins. Eighty per cent of life energy is given to us by the Sun.

The Earth silently provides us with all the basic raw material, minerals, green vegetables etc. It also gives us Spiritual, Divine, Medicinal and herbal plants, fruits and shaded trees. It silently gives mankind a range of life saving material without any discrimination of caste, creed and religion.

It is a misconception that 'Nature' is hostile to man. If approached in true harmony, its secrets can be revealed and the energies harnessed for the benefit of living beings.

Discover your divinity, find your unique talent, serve humanity with it, you can generate all the wealth that you desire.

When your creative mind matches the needs of your fellow humans, then wealth will spontaneously flow from the unmanifest into the manifest. You will begin to experience your life as a miraculous expression of divinity and you will know true joy and the art of blissful living.

Your very self is an ocean with a fortune of undiscovered wealth deep inside your mind, and unbounded love that you can offer to serve humanity. Your ageless mind is so powerful that you can create any situation or any environment of your own choice around you.

The greatest discovery of mankind is that a human being can alter or mould his life by altering his attitude.

–6–

Mantra, Yantra and Tantra

The Sustainable Habitat is the culture of building a playful and joyous internal as well as external environment. Like any culture, it expresses life and grows over a long span of time. Design is to be seen, felt, perceived, conceived and experienced.

The Sustainable Habitat concept describes creation in two basic phenomena - Purusha and Prakriti.

PURUSHA is consciousness, the life source. It is also called Atman. The Paramatman or Vaishwanara (the universal consciousness), the Atman (individual consciousness), Prana (life) and Jiva (also life or soul).

Atman reflects as Prana or Jiva in the body through the mind. Purusha is timeless, ageless, constant, absolute consciousness. A singular truth—Adwaita. Prana is the central source of all energies in all living things, and not energy itself. Prakriti is the world of name and forms, ever-changing; evolving and operating in Dwaita, the dualism of positive or negative, creation or destruction, good or bad, male or female.

PRAKRITI has countless forms. It also has permanence, but of a different nature. It is in the cyclic relay order *i.e.* while the species survives over the time, the body of the species is created and destroyed and recreated again and again. It is therefore, temporary at a given body level.

After Prakriti comes Purusha, the life source. Purusha manifests itself in Prakriti through Ego and Ambition. Thus Purusha is life, the essence, the idea, the will behind any name from the physical world; in the absence of which, the physical mass, forms or systems simply crumble and decompose. Purusha is the power behind all physical existence.

Three aspects for any activity:
1. Mantra or concept (energy)
2. Yantra or mediums (instruments or tools)
3. Tantra or act of creation (administration)

1. *The Mantra or Concept*

Mantras represent the respective energy networks. Each Yantra has its mantra as well as icon. All yantras evolve patterns from a central point. This centre is considered the source of creation and the object for concentration. The concentric patterns around the centre are specific to the energy pattern one wishes to invoke. This pattern is a visual code to constantly remind the sadhaka of the network he is meditating on.

2. *Yantra or Mediums*

Yantras are for the intellectually superior or evolved persons who may not need icons.

Yantras are generally two dimensional, symmetric, concentric patterns using elementary geometric forms such as circle, square and other regular geometric polygons. Lotus flowers with the number of petals varying from four to one hundred are also incorporated.

Yantras have colour codes too and can be designed and developed to represent any specific energy network.

3. *Tantra or Act of Creation*

The problem is of the relationship between the sensory organs and the external mind. Both, the mind and the senses should be disciplined and be in harmony and awareness with Prana. Mediums and methods are developed responding to senses and the sensuality of the mind. First and foremost, the mind should have positive reasons and clear objectives to concentrate upon.

Mantra, Yantra and Tantra

Some intermediary mediums to reach the state of stability:

Vehicles or catalysts are developed. These carriers are sound, touch, vision, taste and smell. Since these are the factors of sensory organs, the mediums or vehicles should correlate with the specific objectives. It should have the potential to reach the goal and its directions and action network should be with clear and accurate commands.

Mantras, Yantras and Tantras are developed with these considerations. In Sanskrit these are defined as:
- Protection through mind is Mantra Sound (concept)
- Protection through effort is Yantra Karma (work)
- Protection through crossing (hurdles) is Tantra (management and methods)
- Mantra is for mental conceptual efficiency. Sound (Audial Form) is its vehicle.
- Yantra is for work efficiency. Vision (visual form) is it's vehicle.
- Tantra is for management efficiency. Process is its vehicle.

Similarly, there are specific touch, taste and smells associated with specific mantra, yantra and tantras.

The above three are MEDIUM and METHODS bridging the gap between human WILL and the objectives, designed and developed for various kinds of human desires; Material, Emotional, Intellectual and Vital Bliss.

Yet keeping meaningful contact with the five elements of Nature, Earth, Water, Fire (Sun), Air and Space respectively by Visual, Audio, Smell, Temperature and Taste (perceptions).

Moods, Emotions, Intellect, Vitality, Bliss are psychological and aesthetical dimensions.

The building must be comfortable, strong and must give psychological satisfaction too.

Man, society and culture are subjects. Technology, mediums of construction, tools, land and environment are form givers.

–7–
A Remedial Measure

It has been well established that the Vastu Principles can be easily applied to modern living. However, the Vastu practitioners should have complete knowledge and sufficient experience before they go into the application of Vastu principles.

The principles laid down in Vastu Shastra were obviously formulated keeping in view the cosmic influence of the sun; its light and heat, solar energy, directions of the wind, the position of the moon, the earth's magnetic field and the influence of the cosmos on our planet. The Vastu influence on any type of building and human beings is like the cosmic influence of the sun (solar system) on our ecosystem. It is equally important to balance the placement of the five elements, Earth, Water, Air, Fire and Space.

The system is an admixture of science, astronomy and astrology. It is influenced by the sun, moonlight, heat, the earth's atmosphere, wind direction, magnetic field and gravitational force on human beings. It gives practical guidelines on site selection, its contouring level, orientation of the building in relation to the climatology and micro weather, arrangements of areas / rooms in relation to the different activities of the proposed building, their proportion as well as rituals for successive stages of house building.

Vastu Principles also suggest the living condition and standard in the house arrangements and also plant and machinery layout in factories, business houses and also the placements of furniture layout, internal colour scheme, the sitting and working arrangement, business administration, raw material and finished goods, arrangements for their storage, positioning of boilers, furnaces, transformers, water storage, kitchen orientation and toilet block etc.

In Vastu, North and East directions are given great importance. East is the gateway to the sun's rays. The North is identified as the pole star, the roof of the world.

Energy lines have been found to emanate from the earth's surface by forming a grid around the globe. The energy is oriented magnetically in the North-South and in the East-West direction. These are called Bio Electro Magnetic (BEM) fields and affect human mind and body, since each body cell acts like a radio receiver with its own vibratory levels. We are most affected by these subtle energies in our daily activities, our places of work and sleep where the body is stationary for long periods.

The magnetic field of the earth has significant influence on the human body and the mind itself acts as a magnet with the head, the heaviest and most important part of our body as the North Pole.

While sleeping with the head towards the North, the North Pole of the earth and that of the human body repel each other, affecting the blood circulation, causing disturbed sleep, tension and other connected problems. Vastu strongly suggests never sleeping with one's head towards the North.

The effect of Vastu is permanent, because the earth has been revolving around the sun, in a geostationary orbit for over 400 crore years due to the magnetic effect caused by its rotation.

Due to the magnetic properties of the earth, the magnetic needle of a compass always tends to point towards the North. Since Vastu is based on the permanent magnetic property of the earth with an inclination towards the North, the effect of the Vastu principles also becomes permanent. However, its applications differ from site to site, building to building, city to city based on the climatical conditions.

It is more interesting to know that the genesis of Vastu

A Remedial Measure

principles lies in the nexus between the earth and the sun. Since these two planets are of universal nature and beyond any religion, caste and nationality, the principles of Vastu have also become universal and secular.

Life exists only on planet earth. No other planet in this Universe has life, because the five elements (Earth, Fire, Water, Air and Space) are existing only on this planet and our life is also based on these five elements. Vastu also suggests the balancing of these five elements in the building.

Vastu Purusha

Ancient sages believed that Vastu Purusha exists in each and every plot with His physical posture aligned on North - Eastern tip and the folded legs in the South-West. The entire body occupies the Vastu Purusha Mandala with the abdomen occupying the centre of the Mandala that is known as the Brahm Sthan, which belongs to Lord Brahma.

The Mandala generally consists of 64, 81, 100 or 169 squares (Yogini). Each square represents different applications in relation with the Northern orientation as shown in the diagram.

VASTU PURUSHA - THE DEMI GOD

While designing the building it is advisable that the heavier structures are proposed in the South-Western corners or along with the Southern or Western zones. In view of the fact that all four corners of a building are not equal in nature, the lighter structures should be towards the North-Eastern sides, because the South-West corner is the hottest and North-East corner is the coolest.

Similarly, it is always advisable for the roof slabs to slope from West to East or South-West to North-East. It is also advisable to propose more openings (doors and windows) towards the North or East or North-East considering the prevailing direction of the wind in the area. This can keep the interiors cool. The sunrays in the morning contain more light than heat, and contain Vitamins D and E, which are very good for the bones.

Keeping this in view, the North-Eastern side of the plot should be kept at a level lower than that of the South-West side. This is because the sun's intensity in the North-Eastern zone is prolonged and remains for the longest duration.

Scientifically, the human eye needs more soft light than intense heat (a glare) for keeping eye diseases at bay, thus energising the eyeball's 'Fundus' for their proper upkeep and keeping them healthy.

Similarly, there is scientific proof that the placement of other house activities is recommended as explained below:

Kitchen

The kitchen should be located in the South-Eastern corner of a building after leaving more open space towards the East. The scientific reason for this being, that the morning sun, rising from the east moves in an arc towards the South due to the rotation of the earth and is in a position of vantage to pump Ultraviolet rays into the South-Eastern aspects of the earth. The Ultraviolet rays are capable of cleaning the foodstuff kept in the kitchen, more particularly because of the elements present in the Southern and Western side of walls. The Ultraviolet rays also provide Vitamins E and D, which are very good for the bones. Similarly, the foodstuff also gets additional strength to reinforce the calcium contents in the human system.

Master Bedroom

It is recommended that the master bedroom, other bedrooms and also the dining hall are located towards the South-Western side of the house to achieve cooling in summer and warmth during winters, because of the reason explained above for leaving more open space towards the North-East and less open space towards the West.

The hot breeze generated by solar energy in less open space between the compound and main wall in the southern and western zone becomes hot air, because lighter air goes up and cool air from the North east zones occupies the area. This process of replacing the hot air with cool air is known as the ' Joule Thompson Effect ' (JOTE),

In this process, the hottest air tends to become cooler due to compression of air molecules pressurised by small horizontal openings. This pressure, inducted by small openings coupled with the earth's rotational force automatically pushes the cool air into the openings (windows / doors) in different directions of the house, resulting in the South-West zone getting purified air i.e. the bedrooms, dining room and kitchen.

Similarly, in planning and developing the new city it is advisable that utmost care be exercised while placing high rise structures, large, heavy industrial hubs, mushrooming R.C.C. structures and big Hydro Electric Projects. Any haphazard positioning and crowding of these buildings in a city would definitely attract the formation of heat islands. In this context, the weather conditions on the earth are mainly controlled by the tilt of the earth. A tilt of a few more degrees would adversely affect the weather conditions on the earth. Assuming all scientific probabilities and in view of the fact that the angle of inclination of the arch which is now stabilised at 23½ degree, has the tendency to change slowly varying between the minimum 200 and the maximum 24.50 within a period of about 40000 years. Therefore, the average tilt works out to be 23.25 degree, which, most probably, is the best tilt to maintain good weather conditions for all living creatures on this planet.

It is therefore, suggested that less weight be put in the North-East direction of the earth to facilitate a healthy living environment. Due to these facts, Vastu Shastra insists on following these principles.

Such examples are also available in Vastu Shastra which suggest that water bodies like water storage tanks, wells, tube wells, pumps, ponds etc. should be placed in the North / North-Eastern zones of the site.

The reasons for this being, the earth rotates at a speed of around 465 miles with the curved surface leaning towards the sun at 23 ½ degree and the major mass of the earth distributed in the Northern part of the globe. In order to achieve stability, it is essential to locate all heavy construction towards the South-Western zone and counterweigh it in the North-Eastern zone to maintain the equilibrium on the rotating surface. This equilibrium is achieved by construction of water tanks, wells, pumps, etc in the North-Eastern direction.

During the Vedic period the sages who thoroughly understood the science of Vastu Shastra, put this science into practice by identifying the correct and safe locations for the various famous structures in the shape of temples, hermitages, places of worship and monasteries, particularly those built in the Himalayan regions. These structures were planned within the energy grids and are, therefore, even after thousands years, protected from destruction from earthquakes and other natural calamities.

The prosperity and survival of the buildings constructed in the earlier age gives a variety of results. However, this does not mean that all ancient buildings were as per Vastu principles. It also doesn't mean that the ancient buildings built on the principles of Vastu did well in the past and are still good for habitat. Many ancient buildings are lying unused and in a state of decay for no specific reason.

People living in old buildings sometimes feel that they are not deriving proper results proportionate to their inputs and efforts.

In the Bhagwat Updesh, Lord Krishna advises: "Do your duties sincerely, use all your five senses properly, and leave the fruits to me."

However, in the present times, people lack patience and expect good results immediately, irrespective of the inputs and efforts put in. Very often, we find that there are technical errors in orientation, layout, planning, adherence to climatological norms, construction techniques, selection of building material, lighting and colour, interior décor and layout, orientation of rooms, etc.

Such ignorance of Architectural Planning can be rectified and remedial measures put in place so that one can feel good and comfortable. Practical factors can be incorporated within the same premises by application of the relevant Vastu principles.

–8–
The Science and Art of Living

The ancient Indian science and art was formulated by our ancestors nearly 5,000 years ago. This science contains principles and practices of design and construction of buildings that ensure a harmonious balance between man, material and nature. A mixture of astronomy and astrology, Vastu takes into account the influence of the sun, moonlight and heat, the earth's atmosphere, wind direction and gravitational force on human beings.

'Vastu' is derived from the Sanskrit word 'Vaas', meaning place of residence. It deals mainly with human habitation and houses. Our sages and saints always wanted to ensure happiness and prosperity, not only for mankind, but also for every living being in the world. They showed a serious concern for the happiness and welfare of all to ensure overall peace and harmony.

The sages and saints discovered and recorded various codes and systems for our good living. These codes are recorded in some ancient scriptures like the Vedas and Upanishads. One of the systems they discovered and explained is Vastu Shastra, the Art of Living.

As per Vastu, the shape of buildings, the proportion of the length, breadth and the height, the entrance and the open spaces, play a very important role in life. However, at the same time, it is not wise to ignore architectural and environmental principles.

While designing any building, Vastu advises us to maintain balance of the five elements-earth, water, fire, air and space in their proper place and proportions to keep the occupants of that place in harmony and to allow them to enjoy happiness and peace in the dwelling.

The orientation of the buildings or the plot towards the direction or level of the existing ground, hills or slopes, highways, stationary or running water, rivers, ponds, streams, wells, places of worship, garbage dumps and other places, influences the Vastu of that site with negative or positive energies. The points of energy allow people to work or rest, to sleep or to plan their future.

When we build a structure in an open space on the earth, the space where various types of energy fields flow, the equilibrium is affected. Vastu helps in designing the structure in such a way that a harmonious flow of energy is present in the building and the equilibrium is maintained.

Vastu also gives suggestions for arranging the living conditions in the house, layout and positioning of plant, machinery and equipment in a factory or business house. It also recommends the internal colour schemes and places for different activities, furniture layout, raw material storage, etc.

Ancient Indian Science

The principles of Vastu are applicable universally and are related to the movement of the planets rather than cast and creed of people. It is holistic and universal with it's application, but also changing with the orientation, geography and climatic conditions of a place.

The postulates of Vastu science as enunciated by our saints are correct and scientific but they should be applied with due regard to the geography and climate.

Cardinal directions are absolute in nature. They do not change. However, the level of importance of their effects needs a subtle modification depending on the latitude and longitude of that place. This fact contributes in a big way in deciding the building orientation.

According to the Vastu Shastra, every house is ruled by a Demi-God, the Vastu Purusha. If not appeased, he would destroy the house and bring adverse conditions for the householder.

According to the text Mayamata, the spirit of the building (Vastu Purusha) has six bones, a single heart, four vulnerable points and four vessels. He lies on the ground, his head towards the North-East. He is responsible for good and for bad fortune; hence, the wise must avoid tormenting his limbs with the limbs of the owner of the house. The body of the spirit must be spared in the course of construction. If, through ignorance of the architects, any of its several parts are rendered defective, the master himself is completely ruined.

Man spends one third of his life in his bedroom, one third in another portion of his house and one third at his work place. He develops his family life within the four walls of his house. This shelter is very important in a human being's life. According to Vastu, there are certain important factors to be kept in mind whenever we construct a house.

TIPS ON SLEEPING POSITION

If we take an average life span of 60 years, we sleep for about 20 years on the bed. So Vastu advices not to sleep with the head towards the North, because the human head is considered to be the North of the body and as per the magnetic principles, like poles repel one another. Thus a person sleeping with his head towards the North will have less blood circulation.

HERE ARE SOME OTHER DIRECTIONS FOR SLEEPING:

- Growing children should sleep with their heads towards the East.
- Try using a wooden bed instead of beds with iron or brass frame as metal works as an antenna. Avoid box type beds.
- At night, switch off the mains because it gives out harmful radiation.
- Open all the windows in the bedroom in the morning for about two hours.

- The ceiling temperature of your bedroom should be less than your body temperature or else you may get a headache.

OTHER TIPS:

- The ideal entrance to the house is from the North, North-East or East. Maximum openings in terms of windows and ventilators should be provided in the North - Eastern quadrant to allow positive sunrays. Further, Vastu dictates that lesser windows should open to the West.
- The master bedroom is recommended in the South West part of the house.
- The kitchen should be in the South East of the house.
- Basement should be constructed in the East, North or North - East corner of the proposed building.
- Balconies or projected verandah \ platforms should be proposed towards the North and East side, with the level of the floor lower than that of the general floor.
- The Number of doors and windows on the first floor should either be more or less than those in the ground floor, not equal to.
- In the living room, furniture should be placed more towards the Western and the Southern side.
- All mirrors should be fixed on the North or East walls and not on the South and West walls. Consequently, the wash-basins in the toilet too have to be fixed to the North or East wall.

If you are living in a flat where you are not allowed to make any structural changes like doors and windows; and you feel that there are negative energies emanating from the house, Vastu has simple remedies which you can carry out in consultation with a specialist.

- Hanging or fixing strategic mirrors can help in deflecting the unwanted or unhealthy energies.
- Changing the position of furniture and fittings.
- Changing colour schemes.

- Changing the direction of circulation of wind / air.
- Adding or moving plants inside the house.
- Changing the layout of garden / terrace garden.
- Changing the interior design.

Vastu is the very foundation of architecture and if the foundation is not correct, it will lead to several complications. In this modern age, even with a limited budget, more and more people are benefitting mentally, emotionally and physically by following the laws of nature. However, it is advisable that practitioners or a Vastu consultant must possess good knowledge of architecture before experimenting with the principles of Vastu.

Sunlight and Sun Rays–Sustainers of Healthy Life

ENERGY FROM SUNLIGHT

1. The Sun is the abundant rechargeable energy that makes life comfortable and bestows prosperity on this planet EARTH.
2. Energy from nature is the base of Vastu Science. The whole universe is a dynamic Web of inspirable energy patterns, solar energy and earth energy.
3. Human beings get 90% energy from the sun which is the rhythm of daily life in the form of warmth and light for all actions / reactions for all the life forms of the Universe.

The Vastu Consultant and Architect has, therefore, to conserve energy with climatological response for the overall growth of the inmates living / working in the built space. We have to learn to handle the delicate balance and sensitivities of natural energy, especially the Sun, in the design process so as to produce an environment full of energy.

Life on Earth is under the constant influence of natural sunlight. The world has always recognised the connection with sunlight. It was profoundly recognised by the ancient cultures that they revered the sun as a God and sought its blessing.

SUSTAINER OF HEALTHY LIFE

Sunlight containing Ultraviolet Rays (Invisible form of light) is beneficial to humans, but there are certain adverse effects too. However, let us not jump to the conclusion that God may have made a mistake in giving us harmful Ultraviolet Light and Rays.

It is a misconception that 'nature' is hostile to man. If approached in true harmony, its secrets can be revealed and its energies harnessed for the benefit of living beings.

Nature, man and product are within an evolutionary network guided by performance standards. Architectural beauty is to be seen, felt, perceived, conceived and experienced.

The so-called 'MODERN THINKERS' are looking towards the Orient for desired peace of mind. India is the source; the fountainhead of the vast ancient Vedic knowledge available on this planet. This open secret is relatively unknown. When the Vedic concept is presented through modern high-tech advances, the sublime information becomes available and can be easily understood. This would give a new outlook to the world of architecture, art and sciences in 21st century.

In the Vedic period, people built homes, temples, and hermitages, applying the principles of Vastu, by balancing the five elements with a view to having a peaceful living, offering prayers and to live in common harmony. However, in the modern world, people built concrete clusters, mainly for a high rate of return. After the Second World War, the architectural practice has turned into a race towards the so-called modernisation. Adopting bureaucratic values that have resulted in worldwide pollution, environmental and ecological problems; with no peace of mind whatsoever, under any kind of shelter.

ULTRAVIOLET LIGHT

Ultraviolet Light is an effective treatment for many diseases. Sun therapy is very commonly used as Naturopathy which includes treatment of anemia, gout, colitis, cystitis, arteriosclerosis, rheumatoid arthritis, eczema, acne, herpes, lupus, sciatica, asthma, kidney problems and even burns.

People will have to understand that there are a lot of health benefits to be derived from Ultraviolet Light as enumerated below:-

1. UV Light increases the efficiency of the heart. At the Tulane School of Medicine, Dr. Raymond Johnson exposed 20 people to Ultraviolet Light. In 18 out of the 20 people the cardiac output increased by an average of 39%! In other words, their hearts became stronger and pumped more blood.
2. UV Light reduces cholesterol. In one experiment, patients with hypertension and related circulatory problems were exposed to UV Light. Two hours after the first exposure, 97% of the patients had almost a 13% decrease in serum cholesterol levels.
3. UV Light is an effective treatment for psoriasis. Reports from the National Psoriasis Foundation indicate that 80% of those suffering from this skin disease improve when they are exposed to UV Light.
4. UV Light activates the synthesis of Vitamin D, which is a prerequisite for the absorption of calcium and other minerals from the diet. Robert Neer and Associates conducted a study on a group of elderly persons to determine if extra sunlight would increase their ability to absorb calcium from their diets. The group which did not receive UV rays had 25% decrease in Calcium absorption while the other group receiving UV Rays had a 15% increase in absorption.
5. UV Light increases the level of sex hormones. In a study at Boston State Hospital, Dr. Abraham Myerson found that Ultraviolet light increased male hormones level by 120%. UV Light activates an important skin hormone.
6. UV Light is an effective treatment for many diseases indicated above. UV Light has been found very effective in killing infectious bacteria, including several forms of tuberculosis bacteria.

Today, practically all sources of Ultraviolet exposure are

seen as detrimental to humans. It is well known that tuberculosis was one of the main diseases that were treated by sunshine and many patients were completely cured.

It is very important to know and study in depth the UV Light and Infrared Rays, which we will be discussing in the following chapters, but we must first realise that too much UV light is bad.

We need a basic amount to support life and maintain a healthy immune system. If someone says that oxygen is hazardous to our health we will say he does not understand the gift of nature. Similarly, it is also in the case of Ultraviolet light. People spend most of their lives under artificial lighting and, as a consequence, suffer. They have to understand the benefits of Ultraviolet light.

Sunlight (containing UV) is beneficial to humans and also has certain adverse effects on persons living and working in artificial lighting. The light in most houses looks yellowish and dingy. The wavelengths of light in the orange - pink - red range caused laboratory animals to loose their hair, show excessive calcium deposits in their hearts and develop large, fast growing tumors. It is also found that when animal cells were exposed to red and Infrared portions of the spectrum, their cell walls ruptured and the cell division process (mitosis) stopped. Sunlight consists of a fairly balanced spectrum of colour. Interestingly enough, blue is the wavelength most lacking in incandescent light bulbs. It has been established that ultraviolet light is a nutrient, just like a vitamin or a mineral. Daily allowance for UV Light has, therefore, been recommended just as in the case of Vitamin C.

In fact overexposure to the sun, in conjunction with certain skin types, is a major factor in the development of skin cancer. The solution is quite simple; mild, sensible exposure to sunlight is not only safe, but is desirable. One of the constituents of sun light is ultraviolet (UV) rays. Modern science has made us believe that it causes cancer, cataract, ageing and wrinkles. This blocking of Ultraviolet rays may severely weaken the body's defenses.

What does nature say about solar light? Researchers have to understand the fact that humans have evolved under natural sunlight. Are we supposed to dismiss five million years of evolution because science doesn't understand the supreme wisdom of nature?

According to photo biologist Dr. John Ott, there are strong indications that UV light through the eyes stimulates the immune system. UV light in large amounts is harmful; however in small amounts, UV rays in natural sunlight act as a "life-supporting nutrient" which is highly beneficial.

Sunlight contains different types of ultraviolet (UV) radiations. UV light is classified as UV-A, UV-B, or UV-C depending on its wavelength. UV-A (320-380 NM), directly adjoining the violet end of the visible-light spectrum, is responsible for the tanning response in humans. UV-B (290-320 NM) activates the synthesis of vitamin D and the absorption of calcium and other minerals.

What are Ultraviolet rays?

Ultraviolet rays are an invisible form of light. They lie just beyond the violet end of the visible spectrum of light. The sun is the major nature source of ultraviolet rays. Lightning or any other electrical spark in the air also emits ultraviolet rays. The rays can be produced artificially by passing an electric current through a gas or vapour, such as mercury vapour. Ultraviolet rays can cause sunburn. Overexposure to these rays can cause skin cancer. Ultraviolet rays also destroy harmful organisms and have other useful effects.

Ultraviolet rays have shorter wavelengths than visible light has. A wavelength, the distance between the crests of two waves, is often measured in units called nanometers. One nanometer (NM) equals 0.000001 millimeter (0.000000039 inch). The wavelength of visible light ranges from about 400 to 700 nm. The wavelength of ultraviolet rays ranges from about 1 to 400 nm. The wavelength of Ultraviolet rays determines whether a material they shine on absorbs the rays or transmits them. For example, only Ultraviolet rays with shorter wavelengths can pass through ordinary window glass.

The glass absorbs rays with shorter wavelength, though they can pass through other materials.

Uses of Ultraviolet Rays

Ultraviolet rays with wavelengths shorter than 300 nm are effective in killing bacteria and viruses. Hospitals use germicidal lamps that produce these short rays to sterilise surgical instruments, water and the air in operating rooms. Many food and drug companies use germicidal lamps to disinfect various types of products and their containers.

Direct exposure to Ultraviolet rays with wavelengths shorter than 320 nm produces Vitamin D in the body. Physicians once used sun lamps that produced these rays to prevent and treat rickets, a bone disease caused by the lack of Vitamin D. The lamps are used today to treat some skin disorders such as acne and psoriasis. Some instruments use Ultraviolet rays to identify the chemical composition of unknown materials.

Medical researchers use such instruments to analyse substances in the human body, including amino acids, enzymes, and other proteins.

The Electronics industry uses ultraviolet rays in manufacturing integrated circuits.

Harmful Effects

The sun's shortest ultraviolet rays, those with wavelength approximately below 320 nm, are particularly harmful to living things. Too much exposure to these rays can cause painful eye irritation or eye inflammation. High quality sunglasses protect the eyes from these rays.

Over exposure to Ultraviolet rays also can cause a painful burn. Melanin, a brown pigment in the skin, provides some protection against sunburn. Sunscreen lotion absorbs the sun's burning rays.

Exposure to the sun's Ultraviolet rays over a long period can cause skin cancer and other changes in human cells. Such exposure also can damage or kill plants.

Sunlight and Sun Rays—Sustainers of Healthy Life

Ozone, a form of oxygen in the earth's upper atmosphere, absorbs most of the sun's Ultraviolet radiation. Without the ozone layer, Ultraviolet rays would probably destroy most of plant and animal life.

Scientific Research

Ultraviolet rays originate within the atoms of the elements. Scientists learn about the make-up and energy levels of atoms by studying the rays. Experts also learn about distant stars and galaxies by analysing the Ultraviolet rays that they give off.

Much research has focused on the role of Ultraviolet rays in chemical reactions that break down the earth's protective ozone layer. As the ozone layer breaks down it becomes less effective as a barrier against harmful Ultraviolet rays.

Experiments indicate that bees, butterflies, and other insects can see Ultraviolet light. The reflection of Ultraviolet rays off the wings reveals patterns that help insects identify mates.

WHAT IS OZONE?

OZONE, OH zohn, is a form of oxygen that is present in the earth's atmosphere in small amounts. Ozone in the upper atmosphere is a major factor in making life on the earth possible. But ozone in the lower atmosphere contributes to air pollution. Ozone is used commercially in water purification processes and as a bleaching agent.

Ordinary oxygen molecules have two oxygen atoms. Ozone molecules are three. Ozone is produced naturally through photochemical and electric discharge reactions.

Photochemical production occurs when high energy radiation from the sun strikes the ordinary oxygen in the earth's upper atmosphere and converts some of it to ozone.

Electrical Discharge reactions including lightning and electric sparks from motors, also convert some oxygen to ozone. Ozone is produced commercially by electric discharge in a machine called an ozonizer.

Most of the ozone is found in the upper atmosphere. The highest concentration is reached, depending on the latitude, between 14 and 19 miles (23 and 30 Kms) above the earth's surface. This concentration is 10 parts per million by volume; i.e. 10 parts ozone per 1 million parts air. The ozone layer in the upper atmosphere shields the earth from 95 to 99 per cent of the sun's Ultraviolet rays. Over exposure to these rays is a leading cause of skin cancer as explained earlier.

In the early 1970's, some scientists expressed concern that chemical compounds called chloro fluorocarbons (CFCs) were breaking down the protective ozone layer. At that time, CFCs were widely used as propellants in aerosol spray cans. After the CFCs are released, they slowly rise in the atmosphere. When they reach the upper atmosphere, the sun's ultraviolet radiation breaks them apart. Some of the molecular fragments that result react with the ozone, thereby reducing the volume.

In 1978, the United States Government banned fluorocarbon aerosols for most uses. However, the ban did not affect the use of CFCs as refrigerants or in insulation. Scientists reported early in 1988 that the ozone layer above Antarctica was disappearing at a rate faster than what was expected.

In 1989, an international treaty took effect that limited the production of CFCs.

Most of the ozone in the lower atmosphere is considered to be an air pollutant. It is formed by chemical reactions between sunlight and pollutants already in the atmosphere.

Ozone produced in this manner is a component of photochemical smog. Such ozone can directly damage rubber, plastic, and plant and animal tissue. It may undergo further chemical reactions that produce other damaging chemicals. Exposure to certain concentrations causes headaches, burning eyes, and irritation of the respiratory tract in many individuals.

Ozone has the chemical formula O_3 and a molecular weight of 47.998. Pure ozone is a pale blue gas. It was first detected by means of its sharp, irritating odor, which is often noticed near electrical switches and machinery. The German chemist Christian Friedrich Schonbein discovered ozone in 1840.

What are Infrared Rays?

When the sun's Ultraviolet rays strike or fall on any object or human being on the earth, they produce Infrared rays in relation to its own temperature and the surrounding temperature.

Infrared Rays

Infrared rays are often called heat rays. They resemble light rays but cannot be seen by the naked eye. They behave similar to light rays in both Reflection and Refraction. Any object such as building material, metal furniture, etc made out of a good conductor lessens insulation and emits infrared rays in relation to its temperature.

As an object gets hotter, it emits more and more infrared rays. Such devices as the Sniperscope, which was invented during World War II (1939-1945), can pick up infrared rays from objects that are warmer than their surroundings. This quality of the Sniperscope enables it to 'see' objects in the dark or through fog.

1. Photographers use film that is sensitive to infrared rays in order to take pictures in places where there is no visible light. Doctors use infrared lamps to treat skin diseases and sore muscles. In these treatments, the infrared rays pass through the patient's skin and produce heat when they strike the affected area.
2. Infrared waves lie just beyond the red end of the visible light spectrum. Sir William Herschel, a British astronomer, discovered infrared rays in 1800 by observing the effect of the heat they produced.

–10–

The Use of Ultraviolet Light and Infrared Rays for Modern, Healthy Living

How to use ultraviolet light and infrared rays for efficient building design based on the principles of Vastu.

SOLAR ENERGY

The sun is the greatest source of energy. But its distribution on earth is unequal. Certain places get more of its heat and certain places comparatively less. Why?

We know that the earth is spherical in shape and flat at the poles. The sunrays fall on different places of the earth's surface at different angles. On the equator they fall straight but on the north and the south of the equator they fall obliquely. Because of the straightness of the falling rays, it is very hot at the equator, but as we go away it becomes progressively colder towards the poles.

Naturally, the question arises, why does the obliqueness of the rays reduce the heating effects. This is so because the rays falling obliquely have to travel longer distances in the atmosphere. The dust particles, vapour and other material present in the atmosphere absorb much of the heat contained in these rays. Hence, the longer the distance travelled by the sun's rays, the larger is the absorption of the heat by the atmosphere. Areas receiving the sun's rays obliquely therefore, receive less heat.

Thus, the places on or around the equator are very hot because they receive the sun's rays directly. On the other hand places to the north and the south of the equator are cold because they receive the sunrays obliquely. The level of heat or cold at a particular place is also dependent on the distribution of water, its height above the sea level and distance from the seashore.

Methods of heat transfer:

There are three rays through which heat is transferred:
1. Conduction
2. Convection
3. Radiation

(1) Conduction is the process by which heat is transferred through matter from a place of high temperature to that of low temperature, without transfer of matter itself. If one end of an iron rod is placed in fire, conduction heats the other end.

(2) Convection in the process by which heat is carried from one place to another place by the bodily transfer of the matter containing it. Fluids, whether liquids or gaseous, are generally heated by this process. Convection heats water in a cane placed on a stove.

(3) Radiation is the process by which heat is transferred from one body to another without heating the intervening medium. Out of all the methods of heat transfer, radiation plays the most important part in the transfer of heat in the atmosphere. The sun is intensely hot, the temperature of its surface being estimated at 6000 degree Celsius. About half of the solar radiation heating the earth is reflected back into space.

The atmosphere does not absorb any appreciable amount of the sun's radiation. It is only when the energy penetrates to the earth's surface that it is absorbed and tends to raise the temperature of the ground, which, in turn, warms the layers of air in contact. Thus, the air in the atmosphere is heated, not directly by the sun, but indirectly by the earth.

Solar power can be harnessed only if the sun's rays are concentrated by using a series of mirrors. Solar energy has been tapped to generate electricity, heating homes, providing hot water and hot air for industries. Satellites and space stations tap solar energy.

Solar energy can be tapped only during periods of sunshine. Widespread use of solar energy will depend on technological developments so as to reduce costs and enable storage of power for use during cloudy periods or night. The solar energy would then provide a continuous and abundant supply of power.

Radiation and Insulation

The meaning of Radiation is 'to send out rays'. The quantity of solar heat transmitted to one square centimetre of the earth's surface in one minute is defined as solar constant.

One square meter of the sun's surface radiates energy presumably equal to 100,000 horsepower at the velocity of light. This energy is transmitted as ultraviolet radiation (short waves) and infrared radiation (long waves). Most of this radiation is perceived as heat and only an insignificant part as visible light.

Every 24 hours, the earth completes a rotation around its axis at a speed of 27 kilometres per minute. At the same time, the earth revolves around the sun on a slightly elliptical orbit at a speed of 28.7 kilometres per second. The total period of revolution is equal to 365 days.

The movement of the earth around the sun together with the inclination of its axis of rotation, results in an uneven distribution of light and heat in the various regions of the earth for any given year.

The position of the earth during its revolution around the sun is measured by the angle of the sun's ray in relation to the equatorial plan of the earth. This angle is called the solar declination and varies between 23.5 degree north latitude and 23.5 degree south latitude.

The days of the year when the solar declination reaches these values are called the solstice. The days when the declination is equal to 0 degree are called the equinoxes. In the period of solstice the perpendicular rays of the sun covers areas of the earth that are at the maximum distance to the north and south of the equator. The boundaries of these areas are indicated by imaginary lines on the surface of the earth designating the Tropic of Cancer as the northern limit and the Tropic of Capricorn as the southern limit.

Passing through the atmosphere, the solar energy is dispersed and absorbed, thus greatly depleting the solar radiation of the earth. The thermal conditions of an urban environment are made up of direct solar irradiation (Insulation) and its derivatives-scattered and reflected radiation and ambient air temperature. In regions with hot climates, direct radiation is a factor exerting the greatest influence on urban environments. The action of direct radiation can be greatly moderated by urban planning methods such as water impounding, shading, special landscaping, etc.

With an increase in the elevation above sea level, the intensity of radiation increases on an average by 10% for each 300 metres above sea level.

In large towns and deserts where there is a high dust content in the air, depletion of the intensity of scattered radiation as such is 30% - 45% of the total amount of solar energy reaching the earth. The atmosphere absorbs 15%. Consequently, the depletion of solar radiation by dispersion and absorption for different latitudes of the earth varies greatly. It is primarily determined by the incident angle of the sun's rays. When the sun is at its zenith, the rays, falling vertically intersect the atmosphere by the shortest path. With a decrease in the incident angle, the path of the sun's rays becomes longer and depletion of solar radiation becomes greater.

On the other hand, the surface of the earth has the property of reflecting heat into space.

Temperature conditions of sea and land are by no means identical, moreover, the surface of the land is not heated uniformly since some places are steppe land, meadows and plough land, other places are forests and swamplands. Other places like deserts do not have a soil covering. Vegetative covering darkens the earth's surface thereby decreasing the flow of heat into the soil.

On the contrary, at night, the vegetative covering protects the soil from heat loss. Besides, part of the Thermal energy is also expended on the transpiration of plants. As a result, soils covered with greenery receive less heat in the daytime. During the day, especially in summer, the surface of the ground becomes heated and at night it cools down. The difference between maximum and minimum temperatures is called the daily fluctuation amplitude.

As is known, the heat capacity of water is two times greater than the heat capacity of land which means that under the same conditions for a definite period of time, the surface of the land receives twice as much heat as the surface of water. Besides, when water is heated, it evaporates thus expending a considerable part of the Thermal energy. However, having a greater heat capacity, the sea accumulates more heat than land with the result that the surface of the sea is warmer than the surface of land.

The mean temperature of the surface of seas and oceans exceeds the average air temperature of the planet by 3 degree Celsius.

The annual air temperature cycle for various parts of the world varies greatly, and is largely determined by the latitude of the localities. Depending on the latitude, there are four basic types of annual temperature cycles:
- Equatorial
- Tropical
- Temperate
- Arctic

Insulation is the direct solar irradiation on the earth's surface that exerts a thermal, light and biophysical effect on man's organism.

In this connection, an interesting proposal was made by architect K. Gutchov who recommended a 'solar hour' (direct solar radiation per hour) as a convenient unit of measurement in calculating insulation which takes into account the varying intensity of solar illumination for various times of the day and year. However, only those hours are of value when the sun is at an altitude of not less than 6 degree above the horizon and the angle of its rays to the surface of wall and window is not less than 15 degree.

In the planning and construction of a town, its territory is divided so that buildings will alternate with open spaces (lawns, greenery and water basins). This stimulates the exchange of air and retards overheating. Varying building densities and the character of the topography of the site also causes temperature fluctuations.

In order to lower the heat load, the building pattern should take into account the closely related problems of orientation, insulation, ventilation, building heights and building density.

When buildings are placed on the perimeter of super blocks, it is advisable that the orientation of the street network be agreeable with the position of the sun. In that case, the necessary insulation of the building will depend on the accepted width of streets, building heights and their location along the street line.

Spacing between buildings should ensure the required insulation. Spacing between buildings depends on how the buildings are placed; with their main facades parallel to the street or perpendicular to it.

In hot climates the spaces between the buildings should provide sufficient area for green spaces as a means of protection against reflected radiation. With these conditions in mind, it is inadvisable to place buildings directly on the street line.

Building density also affects the microclimate in hot, humid and dry zones. In the humid pattern, groups of buildings shade each other, which helps in improving the microclimate. Thus, in the first instance, an open layout of buildings on the site is advisable.

A latitudinal position of the larger axis of a building with a deviation of up to 15 degree on both sides (for better insulation) is believed to be the best orientation for many hot countries.

With minimum spacing, buildings will receive maximum mutual shading.

Playing an effective role in the depletion of solar radiation are green spaces. Depending on their density, radiation is decreased by as much as 86% as compared with an open area.

In a tropical climate, it is advisable to provide covered passageways for pedestrian traffic for protection against the sun and rain.

–11–

How to Use Ultraviolet Light, the Gift of Nature, for Our Perfect Health

In light of the explanations given in the preceding chapter, we come to the conclusion that U/V rays with W / L 1 to 300 nm is harmful for human consumption while W / L of 320 nm produces Vitamin D in our body and about 320 to 400 nm is good for human consumption.

The early morning sun's rays pass through the Ozone layer and reach the surface of the earth with lesser radiation. The W/L during the period from sunrise up to 2 hours later is 320 to 400 nm and is good for human consumption. If it mixes with cold water, it multiplies the vitamin capacity and is very good for the human skin and eye and also produces positive energy.

As the sun rises, it comes closer to the earth and the distance of W/L between the crust comes down to lower than 300 nm. Between 10:00 a.m. and 4:00 p.m. the sun emits Infrared Rays. This scientific theory had been discovered much earlier by authors of Vastu and they suggested the placement of five elements and made the following recommendations:

1. Spend at least one hour outdoors everyday without worrying about the weather. Activities that are supposed to be conducted outdoors should not be done indoors. Take a walk outdoors in the fresh air and marvel at the beauties of nature that unfold before your eyes.
Avoid exposure between the hours of 8:00 a.m. to 5:00 p.m. and avoid looking directly at the sun, as it will damage your eyes. While indoors, sit by an open window.

This will provide you with the full visible spectrum of light including the UV and the view of the gardens and greenery outside your window will be relaxing both to the eyes as well as the mind.

2. Wear sunglasses of a neutral grey colour.
3. For those who wear glasses ask the specialists about UV-transmitting lenses.
4. Don't use coloured contact lenses, as they can cause many problems. Use clear white contact lenses.
5. UV-Transmitting Plastic Windows should be considered instead of regular glass, on the South side of the building.
6. Avoid use of Suntan Lotions having PABA. The U.S. Food Drug Administration has concluded that fourteen out of seventeen Suntan Lotions containing PABA can be carcinogenic when used in the sun and can cause genetic damage to the DNA in the skin.

Exposure to Electromagnetic Waves and Electric Radiation

Many people, who work in areas where radiation may be present, use an electroscope as a dosimeter. A dosimeter is a device that measures the amount of radiation to which a person has been exposed. An electroscope must be charged before it can be used as a dosimeter. It gradually discharges when exposed to gamma rays, X-rays, or other forms of radiation. The amount of charge lost shows the level of exposure. An X-Ray technician wears a dosimeter that will change colour if radiation is present.

William Gilbert, the physician of Queen Elizabeth 1 of England, made the first electroscope. He has described it in a book published in 1600.

The Sun's Electromagnetic Waves

Electromagnetic waves are related patterns of electric and magnetic force. They are generated by the oscillation (back and forth movement) of electric charges. Electromagnetic waves travel through space at the speed of light which is 186, 282 miles (299, 792 kilometres) per second.

How to Use Ultraviolet Light

The simplest electromagnetic waves are plane waves. They move through space in straight lines. The strength of the wave varies in space and time with alternating crests and troughs. The distance from crest to crest is called the wavelength.

The electromagnetic spectrum consists of bands of different wavelengths. The main types of electromagnetic waves are in order of increasing wavelength-gamma rays, X-rays, Ultraviolet light, visible light, infrared rays, microwaves and radio waves. Gamma rays are less than 10 trillionths of a meter in length, and some long radio waves measure more than 10,000 kilometres.

All types of electromagnetic waves have the properties of visible light. They can be reflected, diffracted (spread), and refracted (bent).

The direction of the magnetic force in all electromagnetic waves is perpendicular to the direction in which the wave is moving. The direction of electric force is perpendicular to both the direction of magnetic force and the direction of wave motion. The strength of magnetic force always equals the strength of electric force.

The electromagnetic spectrum extends from short gamma rays through light waves to long radio waves. Thus, the spectrum diagrammed below gives the frequency and wavelength for the various waves. Frequencies are given in hertz and wavelengths in meters. The raised figures with the 10's are a way of abbreviating numbers. For example, 10'15 hertz equals 1 followed by 15 zeros, or 1, 000, 000, 000, 000, 000 hertz. The number with a minus sign tells us how many places the decimal point must be moved in front of the number. For example, 10'-7 meters equals 0.0000001 meters.

USES OF ELECTROMAGNETIC WAVES

Doctors use gamma rays, which are emitted by radium, to treat cancer. They also use X-rays to treat cancer and, in addition, to help, locate and diagnose internal disorders.

Ultraviolet rays are used in sun lamps and fluorescent lights and as a disinfectant. Infrared rays, which are emitted by hot objects, are used in infrared lamps to treat skin disease and to bake enamel.

Microwaves are used to cook food. Radio waves are used in radio and T.V. broadcasting.

The technological use of electromagnetic waves depends on the ease with which the various wavelengths can be dictated and produced. Wavelength is related to the vibration rate of electrons in the energy source. Slower the vibration, longer the wavelength. Long waves are the easiest to produce.

The use of radio waves for communication began soon after 1900.

Shorter waves were not effectively utilised until the development of such devices as the Klystron, a type of microwave tube.

Development of the laser during the 1960's provided new uses for short waves. For example, the laser enables Ultraviolet and infrared rays to transmit voice messages and television signals.

–12–
Energies from Colours and Light
(Influence the Mind, Body and Environment Around us)

THE ENVIRONMENT AROUND US

Colours and light are very powerful in influencing the human mind and body. It is also the least expensive, easiest and quickest to use, to change or to create a decorating scheme. Colours and light can change the visual size and shape of a room as well as create an atmosphere and add warmth, vitality and beauty to it and change the mood of the user.

During the Vedic period, all colours were extracted from vegetables and flowers. These colours were more permanent in shade, soothing to the eye and had a natural tint. Even now in many parts of the world, instead of using synthetic colours, vegetable colours are used, particularly in textile printing and making designs, miniature paintings, ceramics, etc. Vegetable colours have no side effect on the skin and eyes.

During the Ice age, the bodies of dead persons were painted red or they painted their bones with red colours. Accordingly, the flow of red blood means the difference between life and death. They probably believed that the colour itself was life giving.

The Egyptians used colours obtained from metal found in the Earth, plants, insects and fishes.

The symbolic use of colour was made at a very early period in human history. During the early period, the heart which was the seat of life, and blood; both red in colour, were identified with life and consciousness.

Yellow was possibly the colour of fire and white depicted day.

If a room has poor daylight, it should be painted in light colours and if it gets a good amount of natural light throughout the day, it can be painted in some deep colours. If a room has a window only towards the North that admits cold light, we should not use blue on the walls.

If a room gets plenty of direct sunlight, it is not advisable to paint the walls yellow and peach. It is always better to have the ceiling in white because a white ceiling reflects light into a room. It is also very important that the temperature of the ceiling is less than the temperature of the human body in order to have a healthy room.

A fluorescent tube light during the day or white colour is harmful for human skin. It also changes the original tint of other colours.

Some coloured lamps and shades produce curious effects. A person's face appears ghastly when seen by light passing through a blue shade, since there is an absence of red and warm tints that produce the normal healthy appearance of the face.

A red carpet will reflect more red rays by artificial light and will appear to be of a stronger red at night than during the day, but a blue carpet is a more intense blue in daytime than in the night. Purple colour contains both, red and blue.

Colour contrast in value is perhaps the most important factor in the composition of a design. Maximum contrast is obtained by the use of colours of extremely strong chromes.

A strong yellow on a black field is an excellent example of maximum visibility. A bright strong yellowish red would be considered as a powerful colour. The colour of an object depends upon the light it emits or sends back to the eye. Opposite contrast colours are quickly changed when mixed, as for black which makes colours both brighter and lighter in looks.

Surrounding an intense colour with grey increases the apparent colourfulness of intense colour making. It appears even brighter or more brilliant. Surrounded by yellow, a grey colour may appear slightly blue. When surrounded by red, it may appear slightly greenish. On the other hand, a grey surrounded by a bright colour may influence the eye to discern in the greying of the complimentary of the bright colours.

One must always bear in mind that no individual is completely white (Purity, Good) or black (Bad), but is an amalgam of the two 'Grey'. A good, sensible blending can create a forceful impression.

Ancient Indian thinkers had rightly recognised the male and female forces, their need for each other for a harmonious co-existence, and, their coming together as equal partners in the process of creation.

All living creatures in the world are believed to be the children of nature, and nature gives multi million colours. A good healthy nation is only possible when we are surrounded by proper colour and light arrangements. In darkness there is only one colour *i.e.* black. Therefore, blending of proper light (daylight or artificial light) with recommended colours is very important.

The white colour depicts day and is opposite to black. It is symbolic with night and death. Right from the past, even today, there has been continuity in the symbolic use of colour. We associate red with parades and games, blue with that of outstanding work, purple as of dignity and reverence, green with nature and healing, yellow with sunshine and, of course, pink to good health.

ENERGIES FROM COLOURS

Colours affect our body and mind to a large extent. The purest and most thoughtful minds are those which love colours the most. Cool colours are sea blue or mainly blue in cast. Warm colours are predominantly red or yellow in cast.

Red makes you feel gay while man can work best when surrounded by blue. However, too strong a blue or red can also become depressing. People often feel cold in a blue room and warm in a red room.

Red is the most popular colour. Next to red in popularity is blue followed by green and yellow. Amongst girls and women, red and magenta red are the most popular colours. Among boys and men, orange or red is more liked. In blue, a woman likes turquoise best and men prefer deep blue.

Dark colours absorb light and heat whereas bright colours reflect light and heat.

Colours For Health

A particular colour can activate or control human glands of different parts of the body functions. Such as, for a good appetiser, or to stimulate a low blood pressure patient, a red family colour atmosphere is recommended. For a high blood pressure patient, an atmosphere with light soothing colours is recommended. Blue is used to control the habit of overeating.

In a hospital, white colour is used basically for hygienic reasons. However, for healing, doctors use green colour in the operation theatre. For good healthy / tasty food, a golden yellow, or tinted brown colour is recommended.

Colours have profound effects on both body and the mind. This fact was recognised centuries back during the Vedic period.

Colour is an energy. You will find yourself drawn to one particular colour more than others. The energy vibration of that colour is what you need.

There are numerous ways to heal and balance with colour. 'Energy follows thought' by concentrating on a particular healing colour; it is the visualization of that colour that will be projected. If we focus on a colour, the energy emanates from our body and begins to change the frequency that resonates with that particular colour.

Colour is light. Light, which is split into **different wavelengths vibrating** at different speeds and at different frequencies. These colours are energies of differing light frequencies and directly affect our body and mind.

Energies from Colours and Light

The object that ABSORBS all wavelengths and DOES NOT reflect is the colour black. Objects that REFLECT all wavelengths and reflect everything are white. Between black and white lies the entire spectrum of COLOURS.

Colours are wavelengths of energy that appear to us as colour because of the potentials and capabilities of the object that either absorb or reflect the energy.

Colour has the ability to influence moods, and can make people feel hungry, contented, excited or calm. Even on a superficial level, colours create physical change and emotional response. It was a popular method of cure even during the ancient times.

Colour is the most powerful decorating element in human life. It is a very personal choice that essentially effects and often commands the very mood of an individual.

If we understand the basics of 'colour', we can create the perfect 'Colour Scheme' that can change the mood from confusion to intelligence or from fear to confidence; with each colour having a profound and direct effect on the individual.

Colours play a very vital role in our modern living. Similarly, pictures, paintings, symbols, decorative items etc. also play a very vital role in generating creative and positive energies.

Research has named as many as millions of colour variations between neutral white, grey and black. A colour attains its true appearance in good daylight. As an observer looks at several colours at the same time, stimulus to his eyes changes and pleasant or unpleasant sensations may result. Yellow light by nature includes most of the spectrum while violet and red, which only include one extreme end of a spectrum, seem dark or very light by nature.

The interior decor in a home can be made pleasing by using a variety of colours, all of which are mixed with entirely complex hues. Greenish-blue mixed with white or with grey makes a beautiful wall colour. Orange against this background will look the best because of it being a complementary colour with which brown furniture will look excellent.

Decorating an interior means fine-tuning of the colour scheme. A bedroom is intended for rest and the colours therefore should be delicate tints or tones; soft, calm and restful. A living room, however, can be more dramatic with a concentration of coloured objects. The baby's room should have pure bright colours because babies can recognise only bright colours. Pink is therefore recommended for the baby's room.

Vastu says that black colour should be avoided in the interiors. Besides a white ceiling, it is good to have at least two different colours on the walls.

The colours used for painting the house should not be loud and jazzy but pleasant to look at. According to the Gods of direction and the colours attributed to them, the colours of the room should be chosen in accordance with the weather conditions.

When any thing is unbalanced, it is due to the colour and by rectifying or correcting that colour we get perfect results. All forces are based on colour. Sunrays reflect seven colours- Blue, Green, Yellow, Orange, Red, Purple and Indigo. There are two other colours, infra violet and ultra violet.

According to Indian Mythology, all colours have their respective Lords.

COLOURS FOR THE EIGHT DIRECTIONS

Vastu is based on the eight directions having individual deities, planets and its own colours as given below:

1. North

Belongs to The God KUBER, who has a store of wealth and prosperity. It is represented by the planet Mercury (Budh) and the colour is Green.

2. East

Belongs to The God INDRA who gives us life, wealth and prosperity. It is represented by the Planet Sun (Surya) and the colour is orange.

3. West

Belongs to The God VARUN who wields power over rain and water. It is represented by Saturn (Shani) and the colour is navy blue.

4. South

Belongs to The God YAMA who has power over justice and death. It is represented by the planet Mars (Mangal) and the colour is red.

5. North-East

Belongs to All Gods and Goddesses who rule this direction and it is the most auspicious corner. The North-East is represented by the planet Jupiter (Guru) and the colour is yellow.

6. South-East

Belongs to The God Fire (Agni). It is represented by the planet Venus (Shukra) and the colour is white.

7. South-West

Belongs to the Demoness, Nairuti (Putna). It is therefore, banned for all auspicious functions. It is represented by the Planet Dragon Head/Tail (Rahu/Ketu) and the colour is grey/brownish with a red tint.

8. North-West

Belongs to Vayu Devta (The God of Wind). It is represented by the planet Moon (Chandra) and the colour is pearl yellow.

RASHI COLOURS

Your favourite colours can be chosen based on the following colours suitable for each Rashi:

	RASHI	SUN SIGN	FAVOURABLE COLOURS
1.	Mesh	Aries	All shades of red and yellow
2.	Vrishabh	Taurus	All shades of white and lighter shades of yellow
3.	Mithun	Gemini	All shades of green and red
4.	Kark	Cancer	All shades of yellow and orange
5.	Singh	Leo	Orange, deep red and white
6.	Kanya	Virgo	All shades of green and yellow
7.	Tula	Libra	Black and lighter yellow shades
8.	Vrishcika	Scorpio	All shades of deep yellow, red and blue
9.	Dhanu	Sagittarius	Yellow and lighter shades of blue
10.	Makar	Capricorn	Blue, violet and deep shades of yellow
11.	Kumbh	Aquarius	All shades of blue, copper and yellow
12.	Meen	Pisces	Blue and light shades of yellow

The Constitution of Most Widely used Colours

Red

The most dramatic and emotional of all colours. The use of red suggests a bold and confident attitude, and is best used in areas that speak of excitement and vivaciousness.

Blue

The only colour that is linked universally to tranquility and calmness. It is often best suited for a bathroom, where one tends to spend much time either in the shower or on the pot which is also a time to relax, and often, to think.

Yellow
A powerful colour, not only in its hue, but also in its effect. It evokes a sense of energy and vitality, and rightly so, in places like the children's room, an art studio, classroom, chamber or a gym.

Green
Represents healing and fertility. Though not very commonly used in residences, it is the perfect colour for new age healing centres, or the meditation room in the house.

Violet
The colour or femininity and emotion; romance and fantasy. Violet on your bedroom walls ensures a good love life and heavenly dreams.

Orange
An amazingly versatile colour that represents warmth, comfort and reassurance. Never really used in its true Saffron Orange hue, the pastel version or peach hue is quite popular for its cool effect on the ambience of a bedroom or study.

COLOUR IS LIGHT

Sunlight and air is the basic element from which all life originates, develops, heals and evolves. The body is a living cell that is stimulated and regulated by light. It has a profound effect on the regulation of human physiological, emotional functioning and the development of our consciousness. Light effectively enhances learning abilities, strengthens the immunisation and plays a role in extension of life. Energies developed by the Sun, Light and Air play a vital role in the formation of the principles of Vastu Shastra.

Sunlight is composed of a variety of energies that are transmitted to Earth in the form of electromagnetic waves. Only a small portion of these waves actually reaches the Earth's surface and the eyes perceive only about 1% of the total electromagnetic spectrum. This visible portion of the electromagnetic spectrum, containing all the colours of the rainbow from violet (with the shortest wavelength) to red (with the longest wavelength) is the most important key to human functioning and evolution. Our lives, health and well being are truly dependent on the sun.

Sunlight is a holistic approach for the development of physiological, emotional and spiritual bodies. The profound human evolution, 'enlightenment' or the portion of the galaxy in which we live is called the 'Solar System'.

Our evolution, in some deep way, is related to our ability to take in and utilise light on a physical and spiritual level. The vision of our sages of the past is no different from the scientific discoveries of the present.

Sunlight, our main source of light, warmth and energy, not only sustains all life on Earth, but also sustains the Earth itself. It provides plants with the energy of photosynthesis, which in turn sustains life on Earth.

−13−
Rhythm of Life with Changing Colours

From sunrise to sunset, environmental colour changes correspondingly affect all living things. The very first sunrise to the sunset of the present, we continue to be awed by the beauty, power, life creating and life sustaining properties emanating from light.

It would therefore, appear that our physiological and emotional centres are synchronised with nature by way of light and that we truly seem to be the offspring of nature. Based on the awareness that daily colour variations in the environment are intimately connected to the body's daily rhythmic changes. Humans have recognised that the seasonal colour changes also reflect biological alterations within all living things.

Harmony within our life processes is related to the level of communication between our body and the environment. Imbalanced responses to specific rhythms, seasons and their associated cycles are related to specific kinds of physical and emotional problems.

Longevity may be related to our ability to integrate and synchronise ourselves with the planetary and solar-stellar energies that surround us. In humans, exposure to sunlight significantly influences physiological and psychological functions. Among these, fertility and mood are two of the most profoundly affected.

Light has played a consistent role in the development of all living things. More recently, Albert Szent Gyorgyi, Nobel Prize winner and the discoverer of Vitamin C, has recognised how profoundly colour and light affect us. From his work, he concluded: 'All the energy which we take into our bodies is derived from the sun.' He saw that, through the process of photosynthesis, the sun's energy is stored in plants, which are in turn eaten by animals and humans take in the oxygen released.

The sun is a source of mental energy. The best minds evolved in a natural process where the sun was temperate; not very hot, not very cold; just the right temperature (+ or -3 degree) of 24 degree Celsius. The hot sun has glare, sharp light and dark shadows. The cool sun has colours and rarely rises above the horizon or often geographically couples with heavy clouds in the sky and snow on earth. It is generally gloomy, but beautiful, with silvery and long hours of twilight.

Hot and humid zones with heavy cloudy sky for long periods of the year also have a distinctive culture and architecture. The sun has played an important role in the development of visual qualities of architecture in terms of textures, colour, roof forms and, above all, in every expression of vitality.

Scientific Discovery

The human body is nourished directly by the stimulation of sunlight; or nourished directly by eating foods, drinking fluids or breathing air that has been vitalised by the sun's light energy. Dr. Zame Kime, in his book *'Sunlight'*, states that a series of exposures to sunlight will decrease the resting heart rate, blood pressure, rate of respiration, blood sugar and lactic acid in the blood following exercise. It also increases energy, strength, endurance, tolerance to stress and ability of the blood to absorb and carry oxygen. The human body is truly a living photocell that is energised by the sun's light; the nutrient of humankind.

Szent Gyorgyi discovered that many enzymes and hormones involved in processing this energy are coloured and very sensitive to light. He added that light striking the body could literally alter the basic biological functions

involved in processing the body's fuel that powers our lives. In 1979, Martinek and Brezin found that:
- (a) Colours of light can stimulate certain bodily enzymes to be 500% more effective
- (b) Some colours can increase the rate of enzymatic reactions and activate or deactivate certain enzymes.

Light not only affects us but our state of consciousness also determines how we use light.

SUNLIGHT FOR OUR HEALTH

Sunlight has been used by all the major historical cultures and it has touched the hearts and creative minds of those who have learned to appreciate its potential. It wasn't until the 1800s that physicians throughout the world became fully aware of the healing properties of sunlight.

At this point in time, cures using light were being claimed for conditions ranging from simple inflammation and paralysis to tuberculosis. It was later discovered that sunlight striking the skin initiated a series of reactions in the body leading to the production of Vitamin D, a necessary ingredient for the absorption of calcium and other minerals from the diet. If Vitamin D is absent, the body will not absorb the amount of calcium required for normal growth and development of bones.

In 1903 Niels Finsen of Denmark was awarded the Nobel Prize for being the first person to successfully treat skin tuberculosis with ultraviolet light. During his many years of work with both sunlight and ultraviolet light, Finsen reported miraculous cures in thousands of patients.

The cosmic cycles affect our universe, which in turn affects the Solar System, which then affects the Earth and so on down through the Earth's climate, seasons and inhabitants, right down to the smallest particle within an atom.

Since all things are integrally connected in this way, everything affects everything else. Nothing escapes this process. Universally occurring variation affects all living things.

Nature has a master plan for us to spend part of our lives exploring our external environments and part of our lives exploring our internal environments.

What the Vedas Say?

It is very important to discuss and discover the indoor environment, particularly in the 21st century, where the environment throughout the world is becoming more and more polluted, in relation to our health, productivity, universal peace and well being in general.

Most of the modern generation spends their working hours indoor, thus eliminating the morning sunlight and fresh air from their daily diets. The absence or imbalance of certain naturally present spectral light components causes a reduction in our physiological, emotional and intellectual functioning. Light, therefore, plays an integral role in the proper biological functioning of all living organism.

In this regard, Vastu play a very important role in helping in creating a clean environment, free from pollution of any kind, full of light and colour needed for the development of a healthy nation with a peaceful environment by balancing the Five Elements of Nature.

Sanskrit Shloka:

Veda says:-

Om Dyauh Shanti Antakrish Shanti Prithvi Shantiraapah Shantiroshadhayah Shantih II
Vanespatayah Shantihvishvedavah Shantihr Brahma Shantih Servagyum Shanti Shanti Revah, Shanti Sa Ma, Shantiredhih, Om Shanti Shanti Shanti Om II

Sanskrit Shloka:

Na Pranena Na Apranena Matyo Jivati Kaschana I
Itarena Tu Jivanti Yasmin Etavapsritau II

Meaning:

Our life doesn't depend merely on the breathing process. The intake of diet is indeed important for health, but health does not rest on food alone, because everything can be thrown out of order if the mind is upset. A turbulence injected into the mind is enough to disturb the entire balance of personality. Your strength is in you. Religion begins where science ends; the beginning of the higher wisdom.

Radiant Energy

Ancient civilisations were apparently aware of light, namely, its route of entry into the body and some of its major effects on the body's regulatory centres and their functions. Major control centres of the body are directly stimulated and regulated by light, to an extent far beyond which modern science, until recently, has been willing to accept.

Though the body's balance is regulated by the autonomic nervous system, which is regulated by the very important part of the brain, the hypothalamus, which receives light energy through eyes, coordinates and regulates most of our life sustaining functions and also initiates and directs our reactions and adaptation to stress.

Many of us spend our lifetime chasing mental images rather than observing the realities of life. The general lack of awareness has already led to the toxification of life's most important basic elements: light, air, food and water.

Light is the major nutrient sustaining all life and it follows that poor and / or incomplete lighting will significantly affect every aspect of human existence. It is important to initially look at the constituents of sunlight as well as the kinds of artificial light to which we are exposed in our daily lives.

Light is composed of waves of radiant energy. Sunlight, which contains all the different wavelengths, provides the total electromagnetic spectrum under which all life on this planet has evolved.

Until 1879, when Edison perfected the light bulb, people spent most of their time outdoors and received adequate daily doses of natural full spectrum sunlight. The light bulb became largely an 'indoor event', which drastically reduced the amount of time to which people exposed themselves to full spectrum sunlight.

Since most of us spend our working hours indoors, eliminating sunlight from our daily diets, it is important to find this indoor environment in relation to our health, productivity and in general.

–14–
Vedic Vastu

The term Vastu is defined as Vastu Kala, the art of designing a healthy building, or a place where living beings reside peacefully. It is presided over by Vastospati, the steady one, The King of Gods, Indra. So, before a house is built, oblations are offered to Indra (wielder of the thunderbolt), Varuna (Lord of rains), and Vayu (Lord of winds). Man builds to seek shelter from these powerful forces. Since Yama (Lord of Death) also rules the world, he too is to be invoked when man builds his small world. In the Vedas, there is a special veneration of the central post, for it is considered a symbol of the Vastospati.

Perhaps, this is an extension of the ancient habitat under a tree that, in the most primitive house, led to the structure being built over and around a central post. The raising of the Vamsa (beam) over the Sthuna (post) is a sacred act during which hymns from the Atharvaveda are recited. The tenets of Vastu thus considered the building of a house as a religious act. A man's private expression—his house—if built according to the traditional Vastu principles, would enrich his public life by bringing him prosperity and contentment.

The Vastu Shastras are a record of these oral traditions that were, in ancient times, best known to the Sthapaties (architects). The shastras incorporated the course of the sun, the moon and the other planets, thus symbolising recurrent time cycles within a house. The house was located correctly in space and time as it incorporated the mathematical and physical science of Astrology.

Texts like the Arthshastras also included the concept of byelaws by describing the position of drains, boundary walls, well/tube well openings and gateways. Spaces between houses, the location of openings in a house, façade treatment and even sanitary regulations were specified. The violation of these laws was punishable by the state, which is more than can be said about modern building byelaws.

Some broad principles can be identified that even today guide the design of the house. These apply to site selection, site planning, the house plan, openings, structure and proportions, set back ratio of open space and covered area etc.

SITE SELECTION

The best shape for a plot is square or rectangular. A triangular site or one with an odd number of corners is to be strictly avoided, though adding a small additional side can amend this. A four-sided plot, tapering to the North-east is the best site.

A site is considered propitious if it drains water from the South-West towards the North-East. However, since most urban housing sites are rectangular, their obstruction can be amended.

Site selection today does not usually involve any pundit. Various other tests mentioned in the Grihyasutra, primarily for determining soil quality are rarely performed today, as the building material comes from areas that may be far away from the site. Poor soil quality can be easily compensated.

The Site or Plot

The site or the Vastu is regarded as the body of a Demi-God, the Vastu Purusha or Vastunara, subjugated by the Gods.

Each victorious God holds down a part of this demon so that he would never rise again.

The Gods, as well as the Vastu Purusha himself, have to be propitiated while building a house. It is said that the Vastu Purusha requested Brahma to always occupy the centre of his being, the nabhi or the navel. Interestingly, Brahma also represents the third dimension above ground level, while Vasuki is the God of the depths.

The Vastu Purusha's head faces North-East while his feet are towards the South-West. Consequently, the North-East portion of the site has assumed a sacred status and is given a great deal of importance during planning. Eight main Gods of the eight cardinal directions inhabit the Vastu, while the Padas or the divisions between these cardinals have a measure of influence on the design process. However, the lesser Gods are not considered unless a person goes in for elaborate sculptural decoration of his house.

The Vastu Purusha Mandala is a square yantra, a diagram, representing the ritual form of the Vastu Purusha. It seeks to represent the microcosm, the essence of all things, the Supreme Being, the Purusha. The mandalas can be of various divisions or padas. There were 64 pada mandalas for religious places, palaces of the kings and towns, 49 pada mandalas for wells, tanks and ponds and 1,000 pada mandalas for forts and cities.

The Agni Puran mentions a 3,400 pada mandala for a country.

For planning a house, 81 pada mandalas were used and the length of the purusha recommended was 120 angulas (1 hasta = 24 angulas = 7.5 feet). Today, while the fundamental principles of the mandalas are not strictly adhered to, they nevertheless provide a useful grid for planning the location of various activities in a house.

The site is planned according to the divinity associated with the padas. The house is usually located on the South-Western side of the site. While the animal sheds are situated on the North-West. The preferred location for the underground water tank or well is at the North-East, which is an indication that water is considered sacred.

According to the Shastras, while constructing a house a minimum amount of open space should be left on the South and the West sides of the site while the North and East should have maximum open space. However, the introduction of bye-laws on a site with restricted amount of space can cause problems in a South or West-facing site. For instance, in order to follow a building bye-law that specifies a 10-foot frontage, this principle has to be contravened, in the process losing the coveted backyard, though gaining a front yard. Fortunately, people are not such sticklers for privacy today as they were in the olden days.

Trees and Plants

The Grihya sutra also mentions the position and types of trees to be planted on the site. The basic rule followed today is that of planting the tallest and shaded trees on the South-West section of the site and shorter shrubbery on the Eastern sides. Since the sun is in the South at midday in a hot climate, tall trees that provide ample shade are grown on the South-Western part of the site. When the sun sets, its angle is low and the shaded trees serve as a useful shading device on the South and West sides. Seasonal flowering plants are recommended on the North-East or Eastern side of the site.

Planning as per Vastu

While a square house is considered auspicious, most geometrical shapes can be allowed in special circumstances. One of the stipulations is that the corners should not be cut, as this is considered inauspicious and attracts evil spirits. In any case, corners are structurally awkward and should not be tampered with.

The divinities associated with the cardinal points play a significant role in the planning of the house. Since the North-East represents the gateway to heaven; the Pooja room and the kitchen must be located in that part of the site. The kitchen should be placed on the South-East, but the gas stove (agni) must face East. The West represents darkness (Varuna), and the South, Yama, Lord of death. The south west is dedicated to Pitra (ancestors) representing exit from life. This corner is considered an ideal location for the master bedroom-(at the feet of the Vastu Purusha). Toilets or the master bedroom should not desecrate the sacred North-East corner.

The center of the house, the garbh griha, the womb of the higher self, has a special significance, especially in a geometrically centralised space. This could be symbolised by using an open courtyard or a tulsi manch. The skylight symbolises this womb. However, these rules are not binding and the ultimate choice of location is left to the master of the house, depending on the condition of the site, its orientation in respect to climatology and micro-weather.

The basic grid locates the sleeping spaces on the South and West, the living space on the South and the cooking and dining spaces on the South-East. The staircase must face East or West, never North, possibly a mythical association where North South was associated with night and death. However, certain modifications have been negotiated these days by making the first step face East or West, so that a person starts climbing while facing East or West. The number of stairs should be odd in number, never even in number.

Openings of Doors and Windows

The total number of doors and windows must be even. Doors are assigned a special symbolic value in the Grihya Sutra. A door on the East brings peace, fame and strength, on the North children and cattle and on the South wealth and fame. A door on the West is to be best avoided as it brings misfortune (evidently, any spillover of activity on the Western side of the house was not considered good for its inhabitants).

If the front door is on the South it must be on the centre line of the house. It should also be the first in a sequence of doors leading to the back door-all on the centre line. Considering that the breeze usually comes in from the South, this is a good way of ensuring cross-ventilation.

Structure

The trabeated structure of the post and beam was deemed worthy of veneration in the Vedas. The posts were especially important as they were compared to Gods in the support that they afforded. A thousand pillared hall, therefore, was considered sacred.

Each post in conjunction with it's cardinal point took on a symbolic value. The Eastern post represented truth and faith, the Southern post, sacrifice and gifts, the Western post, strength and power and the Northern post, brahmins and kshatriyas.

This symbolism was extended to other parts of the structures as well. The pinnacle represented fortune, the chief post law, the doorjambs day and night, while the foundation represented the bull and the ocean.

The only rule that modern Vastu advisors insist on is that the South-Western corner must have the maximum height and the North Eastern corner the minimum height. This is an extension of the basic rule of the site having its highest point at the South-West and lowest point at the North-East.

In its widest sense, Vastu was anything made with skill. This applied not only to houses, buildings, temples and towns, but also to roads, drains, ponds, wells, furniture and ornaments. It offered a multi-disciplinary approach to the process of design. This, perhaps, is what we must learn from Vastu Shastra to provide a framework for design that maintains the required standards, proper shape, proportioning systems, a proper cross-ventilation, a suitable light and colour blending to be in tune with the human mind and brain.

Planning the Buildings as per Vastu Shastra

The body-mind is an auto-system. Man takes his sustenance, growth and development from nature.

Man has various existence roles. For each of his role, he has environmental needs to live or perform these roles. He wishes to perform each of his activities in his own way. He has his own ways of ENJOYING work or acts (joy of doing something). His own SANCTITIES, the way he sleeps, bathes, eats, works as a 'self', an individual, family, institution etc.

There are over tones and priorities of various issues such as Physical, Material, Emotional, Traditions and Taboos, Aspiration, Status or Anonymity, Intellectual etc. Thus the simple act of Sleep, Eat, Cook, Meet, Sing and the other thousands of every day activities have various environmental needs, desires or aspirations which give different meaning to different people. 'FUNCTION' and 'ACTIVITIES' thus assume a much wider meaning.

In the individual buildings or rooms too, the functional spaces are of various kinds.

In India, building designs vary significantly from place to place. Regional and sub-regional differences in house design and building systems are quite obvious to the eye. There are flat roofed houses built in stone in Rajasthan and sloping roof structures in bamboo in the North-East. The diversity exists in all directions. It is the result of technical soundness, affordability and ultimate appropriation of a building system by a large number of people.

Some very obvious conditions that lead to diversity are:
1. Living standard, spatial and functional requirements.
2. Climate and Micro-Weather condition.
3. Economic conditions of house and community.
4. Material and energy resources available.
5. Local building material available.

Utilisation of available materials and energy resources in an area is something that building technologists have much greater control over. They can choose from existing resources and techniques of construction or develop new building materials, products and processes from locally available material. They have the option of enlarging the resources base by importing material from outside the locality.

Building activity can also develop into a rural industry and contribute to the economic well-being and development of an area. The choice of Vastu Technology is important in housing and thus developmental concerns must not be forgotten.

Housing is people's activity. We must recognise that it exists as a system today with its own dynamics. It is, however, a relatively unhealthy system and therein lies the problem.

People are forced to resort to other solutions from within

the confines of their limited resources and abilities. The solution for improving the state of shelter lies not in re-designing the housing system, but we need to trigger off a process of technical selection and upgradation as a result of which building systems are developed, keeping in mind the natural resources within the parameters of the Vastu system.

–15–
Practical Vastu Tips and Simple Remedies for a Healthy Environment

Due to ignorance, there may be violations of Vastu rules; the ill-effects of such violations have to be suffered by the owners/occupiers or users of those premises. It may also be noted that ill-effects of some negative energies are suppressed by the good effects (positive energies) of so many other good aspects of Vastu or vice versa.

It is, therefore, necessary to identify with the help of a Vastu expert the defects and demerits in the site and construction and/or in the building, as soon as possible, and get them rectified.

As a Vastu Consultant, I have come across many instances where a number of my clients have gained much and have improved their conditions by making the necessary amendments and alterations in their houses, industries and business premises, in accordance with the principles of Vastu.

Different Vastu rules are applicable depending upon the orientation of the site, location and purposes of use etc. in accordance with climatology and micro-weather condition. A rule that applies to one particular site at a particular location may not necessarily be appropriate and applicable to another site in a different location.

Vastu for Modern Living

Nowadays, people have again started believing in Vastu Shastra and even the most modern building whether it is a house or a multi-storeyed commercial building, hospital, hotel, restaurant, business establishment, small or big industries are being planned in accordance with the principles of Vastu.

Even in other parts of the world, architects and builders are following the principles of Vastu in their design.

The Chinese people are also firm believers of the Vastu principles in the form of Feng-Shui.

Feng-Shui is an extremely ancient and well-developed system dating as far back as approximately 500 years ago. Today, in Hong-Kong, Singapore, Taiwan and other Far Eastern Countries, the most modern buildings are designed and decorated adopting this ancient system.

One must possess sufficient knowledge of Vastu Vigyan (Science) and its application before advising or designing one's place of residence or work.

Part I: Practical Vastu Remedies for Modern Houses

1. The basement should be constructed towards the East, North, or North-Eastern Corner of the proposed building
2. Balconies or projected verandahs/platforms should be proposed on the North and East side, with the floor level lower than that of the general floor
3. Terrace or a part of terrace should be in the North-East or North or Eastern sides. It should never be towards the South-West
4. All the below-mentioned places are recommended on the North-Western corner of the plot or house. However, care should be taken to ensure that they do not touch the boundary walls in the North and Eastern side of the building:
   (a) Car Garage
   (b) Out Houses
   (c) Servant's/Staff rooms
   (d) Kennels
5. Open portico can be proposed towards the North-East and Eastern side of the building
6. Set back or open spaces should be proposed towards

the East and North side rather than towards the South and West side of the plot

7. Thicker walls should be constructed in the South and West side of the building, and thinner walls in the East and North side
8. Mezzanine floors or lofts should be built on the Southern or Western side of the hall, or house as the case may be
9. Number of doors and windows on the first floor, should either be more or less than those in the ground floor and not equal
10. In a R.C.C. framed structure, the number of columns or beams should be even and not odd
11. The height of the building from the ground should be such that the number of risers should be odd *i.e.* 3,5,7,9 respectively. If you propose risers of any staircase as 6" in height, then keep the plinth height of the building 1'6" or 2'6" and not 1' 0" or 2'0" so that the number of steps (risers) come up to 3 steps. Similarly the height of each floor should be such that the number of risers (steps) remain odd

    Vastu explains that while climbing the staircase, only the right foot should touch the first floor of the house/ building
12. Doors, windows and other openings can be on the North-East corner of the building or the room rather than on the West or South side
13. No garbage should be dumped in the North-East corner of the building. The North-East corner should always be kept clean and free of junk
14. The shutters of doors should be single and not double. It should open towards the left and not to the right
15. The Pooja room should be in the North-East. The kitchen should be located in the South-East; the Master Bedroom should be in the South, West or South-West corner. Newly-wed couple's room should be in the North-West corner and young children's room in the East

16. Level of the floor in the North-East should be lower than that in the South-West
17. The North-East boundary wall should be lower and of thin or light material and the South-West boundary wall should be higher and thicker as compared to the North-East side of the building
18. Underground water tank is recommended on North-East corners
19. Bore well, tube well and other water bodies, fountain, swimming pool etc. are also recommended on the North-East corner of the plot

Vastu Tips for Modern Bedrooms and Office Planning

Let us discuss the most important part of Vastu Planning for positioning of the bedrooms in a modern residence/house/Flat.

WHAT IS A BEDROOM ?

The bedroom is a place where a person keeps his/her personal belongings, changes and dresses up according to the social engagement, official work or in casuals.

Married couples use the room to start a family, give birth to children, apart from the most important function of the bedroom: Rest and sleep soundly for approximately 8 hours and wake up the next morning totally refreshed and fully charged with new energy.

The bedroom is the one portion of the home where one spends a maximum portion of his life; irrespective of a big house or small house, a guest house or a palace or a hotel, or a motel, or even a dharamshala or ashram.

It is the place where a person sleeps or rests for at least 8 hours. This means that we spend almost 1/3rd of our life in the bedroom. This means that if, as an example, a human being's average life is taken as 60 years, he or she spends 20 years on the bed. And at least another 10 more years he or she spends in the bedroom in the morning after waking and in the evening before sleeping.

This explanation convinces us that we spend almost half of our average life; 30 years; in the bedroom.

We spend another 8 hours at our workplaces and offices, which amounts to another 20 years of our life. Assuming an average life span of 60 years, this means that we spend 30 years of our life in the bedroom, 20 years at the workplace and the balance 10 years in other activities like travelling to the workplace, marketing, social activity outside the house, family activities within the house in places like the verandah, lobby, drawing/dining room, kitchen, study, hobby room, watching T.V., listening to music, interacting with the family etc.

During my architectural and Vastu practice of more than 50 years, I have carried out a lot of study and research in the area and am convinced that we, as architects and Vastu advisors, should give maximum attention to the planning of bedrooms and offices for our modern living.

Vastu Tips for Planning of Offices

Description of an office or work place

An office or work place is such where a person concentrates on his job, takes the right and quick decisions and gives output with more efficiency. A person who can do this effectively is a successful person and rises in his job. This is only possible when the office / working environment is good and full of positive energy. Very often, we find that these days, people in the office or work place are confused or get tired or make mistakes.

I would like to advise my clients, students, friends and general public to carefully study the following two Parts (Part II and Part III).

In these parts, I have attempted to give a logical, compounded solution with examples.

Part II-Modern Bed Room and Its Internal environment with recommended sleeping positions.

Part III- Internal Office Environment with Seating Position.

Part II: Vastu Tips for Modern Bed Rooms and their Internal Environment with Sleeping Positions

Let us first discuss the negative aspects of modern bedrooms.

Most of our architect friends plan a house without giving much importance to the orientation in respect to the micro weather conditions and climatic parameters. The master bedroom and children bedrooms are placed in such a way that hardly any solar energy enters the bedroom.

Moreover, neither is there is any natural light in the rooms, nor is there any proper air circulation or cross ventilation. The quality of air and natural light is very poor with the suitable sun energies, as a result of which, these types of bedrooms are mostly unhealthy to live.

Furthermore, with the modern living style, we cover the flooring with wall-to-wall synthetic carpets. The walls are painted with synthetic plastic emulsion paint. The terrace roof is covered with synthetic polythene or 3-4 layers of tar coal with hot bitumen poured for waterproofing.

This process chokes the breathing of the natural building material, as a result of which, we feel that we are living inside a plastic bag.

For increased air conditioning effectiveness, split air conditioners are installed, and all the windows and doors are sealed to make them air tight. As a result, the room recycles the same stale air and fresh air is not allowed to enter the room.

We may derive a temporary feeling of comfort in a sealed off air-conditioned room. However, try and imagine how long you can live a healthy life in this kind of atmosphere? Are we not reducing our precious life span?

The most important and dangerous point which is not visible to the naked eye, is the Electromagnetic and Electrical Radiation omitted (emitted) in the modern living bedrooms by all sorts of electrical gadgets such as T.V sets, music sets, V.C.R., hands free telephones, cell phones, computers, fax machines, electric coffee/tea kettles, heaters, air conditioners, foot or body massagers, etc.

Electronic Radiations are invisible but are important hazards causing several problems to the human health and comfort.

In Modern Architecture, concealed electrical wiring is laid down in PVC pipes (instead of 16 gage SWG conduit pipe with proper earthing) of three phase or four wire system, resulting in PVC pipe wiring when voltage and current passes through the conductor. EMF is ensued. Moreover the fashion is to use 4' fluorescent tube light in the bedroom just above your head close to the wall. These again create an invisible health hazard.

Scientists are finding co-relations between exposure to Electromagnetic radiation and immune-system disorders like chronic fatigue, EMF sensitivity syndrome (a constellation of symptoms that include an inability to concentrate, skin rashes, muscle weakness, mild panic, disorientation, headache, visual disturbances and feeling of faintness etc).

Modern bedrooms are furnished with beautiful furniture made out of metals like brass, steel, wrought iron, which works as an antenna in between EMF and radio transmitters, communication equipment and your body.

Generally, box type beds with long steel hinges are made for using as storage space to reduce the cluttering in the room. People tend to dump all types of junk in the bed box resulting in heaviness or headache and bad dreams.

Sometimes, out of sheer ignorance, people sleep with their head towards the North. This sleeping posture is very much against the principles of Vastu and results in reducing the supply of blood to the brain.

Orientations of windows, their size and direction of opening are very important factors and should be in accordance with the direction of the Sun in relation to the weather and climatic condition.

The interior décor, colourly of the walls, lighting arrangement and pictures or paintings on the walls have to be very carefully chosen according to the mood, style and health structures of the occupiers of the bed room and in conjunction with his status, age and profession.

Recommended Sleeping Positions

The orientation of the bed, posture, direction of the head and feet is not only very important for a healthy and peaceful life, but also for sound sleep.

The most important principle of Vastu Science advises to NEVER sleep with the head towards the North. The human head is considered to be the Northern tip of the body, and sleeping with the head towards the North causes the magnetic forces of the body and the North Pole to repel each other resulting less blood circulation to the brain. Scientists have proved that the magnetic field of the North Pole is stronger as compared to that of the South Pole.

The human body is a good conductor and the blood also contains iron. As a result, the Earth's Magnetic Field and Electromagnetic field (EMF) directly affect the human body and mind.

The recommended sleeping positions for sound sleep and healthy body and mind are as follows:

- Persons with low blood pressure should keep their head towards the South-East or South
- Persons with high blood pressure should keep their head towards the North-East or East
- Persons with breathing problems should keep their head towards the North-West
- A professional person selling his brain should generally keep his head towards the South-West or South. (A deep study is required to get better results for different professions. Experts should be consulted before deciding the appropriate position)
- A businessman (trader) should keep his head towards the West
- A businessman (manufacturer) should keep his head towards the West-South
- Retired persons should keep their head towards the North-East or East

- A new born baby's head should be kept towards the South
- Growing children's head should be kept towards the East
- A pregnant lady should NEVER sleep with her head towards the North or South. The best position is with the head towards the West. If she does not feel comfortable, she can sleep with her head towards the East

These recommendations are generally for a normal situation. For specific problems or diseases, or for different professions or job and the environment around or the EMF energy in the room or building structure and orientation of the building in relation with the weather condition and surrounding, one should consult an expert.

Design and Shape of the Bed

- The bed should be rectangular, without an attached side table. Round shaped bed is not recommended. A single bed should be without a box.
- Beds should be made out of seasoned wood. Never use beds made out of iron or brass or any other metal or tubular frames as the metal frame works as an antenna. In case use of a metal bed is unavoidable, a proper earthing must be provided for the metal frame.
- Box type beds should be avoided. If a box is essential in order to save storage space, use only small brass hinges that also act as an antenna under your body. Never store leather or metal items in the box as they lead to bad dreams. Store only bed sheets, blankets etc in the box.

Fittings and Fixtures in the Bedroom

- T.V. set is not recommended in the bedroom, if must, than keep the T.V. set a minimum of two meters away from the bed.
- All electrical and electronic equipment like music system, computer, or any other electrical gadget must be kept at a minimum of 1.5 meters away from the bed. When not

in use, it should be ensured that the equipment is switched off from the mains and not by the remote.
- The internal wiring, particularly in the bedroom and attached bathroom must be concealed in a 16 SWG conduit pipe of proper size and dimensions. Both ends of the conduit pipe along with the switch box made of M.S. Sheet or CI must be properly earthed. PVC pipe wiring should be avoided.
- Avoid florescent tube lights in the house particularly in the bedroom. Ordinary bulbs of proper wattage must be used.
- Avoid split type air conditioners. Use window type air conditioners and always keep the fresh air vent in the open position.
- Open all bedroom windows in the early morning for a minimum of two hours and allow proper circulation of fresh air and cross ventilation in the room.

Paint

- Avoid the use of synthetic paint and synthetic material like plastic emulsion paint, synthetic wall-to-wall carpet or synthetic sheet on the roof for water proofing in the bedroom. These synthetic materials choke the breathing of the walls and ceiling and gives us a feeling of living in a plastic bag. Normal distemper or white wash and soft, pleasant colours should be used on the walls. This has also been explained in the previous chapters.
- The temperature of the ceiling in the bedroom must be less than the body temperature, otherwise it will cause headache.

Beams and Columns

- Avoid any type of hanging RCC or steel structural beams on the roof. There should not be any columns in the bedroom.
- All corners of the bedroom should be at an angle of 90 degrees. Cut corners are not recommended in the room.

- Putting up of mirrors on the wall or at the bedside should be avoided.
- Windows and doors should be positioned in accordance with the orientation of the room considering the climatic and weather conditions.
- Paintings, photographs or calendars should be of pleasant colours and of figures that give positive energy and happiness to the occupiers of the room.
- Avoid any type of horror pictures like human or animal skeletons, dead animal heads or skin, dragon or photographs of dead bodies of human or animal. Disfigured, broken or partly broken statues of God or Goddess idols should not be kept in the house.
- Keep fresh flowers of your liking and / or live fresh plants in the bedroom. Avoid synthetic plants or flowers.
- Puja corner or puja place should not be in the bedroom. If there is no alternative, it should be at a height of more than 4 feet above the floor level. Shoes must be kept outside the bedroom.

COSMIC ENERGY IN THE BEDROOM

Sunlight and fresh air are the basic elements from which all life originates. Our body is a living cell; it has a profound effect on the regulations of the human physiological and emotional functioning and the development of our consciousness.

Proper sunlight and good quality of air plays a very important role in the extension of a healthy life. The rhythm of life changes from sunrise to sunset and is composed of a variety of energies that are transmitted to Earth in the form of electromagnetic waves.

If only small portions of these waves, ultraviolet rays, light and radiation are properly and very carefully utilised in the bedrooms is a most important key to play a vital role in formation of principles of Vastu Shastra.

Scientists have discovered that the human body is nourished directly by the stimulation of sunlight or nourished indirectly by drinking, eating food and breathing fresh air.

The Vastu Principles strongly suggest that all bedrooms must have proper sunlight and fresh air of good quality.

Part III: Vastu Tips for Internal Office Environment with Seating Positions

- Keep the office table close to the West or South wall of the office room
- Sit facing towards the North, East or North-East
- Office table and chair should be made out of seasoned wood
- Steel or metal furniture should be avoided
- Avoid using fluorescent tube lights
- The colour of the walls should be soft and in natural shades. Try to use off white colour on the ceiling and the walls. Dark shades should never be used
- The general lighting should be sufficient, bright and pleasant. No light should give any glare to the eyes
- Natural daylight should be perfect from the North, East or North-East
- Avoid using reflecting mirrors on the table top or on the walls
- Pictures or paintings should be matching with the mood and should give positive energy so as to improve work efficiency
- Computers and other electronic equipment should be kept at a distance of 1 meter from the seat. When not in use, all the equipment must be switched off from the mains.

Part IV: Vastu Remedies for Modern Flats

If you are living in a flat where you are not allowed to change the structure or position of doors and windows; or having fixed designs activities like kitchen, bathroom etc. and you are not feeling happy or healthy, Vastu has simple remedies, which can be tried. The results of such remedies also turn out to be good.

Practical Vastu Tips—Heathy Environment

SOME VERY SIMPLE REMEDIES:

- Hanging / fixing strategic mirrors on the North and Eastern wall to deflect unwanted or unhealthy energies
- Repositioning the furniture and fittings
- Changing colour schemes and lighting
- Changing the direction of wind/air circulation
- Adding water bodies or fountains towards the North or North-East
- Adding or removing plants in the house
- Adding or removing or changing the position of electrical equipment in order to alter the energy flow
- Changing the layout of garden/terrace garden
- Adding/removing partitions
- Changing the position of the bed/seating arrangement/ cooking gas and burner, jewellery box, safe etc.
- Changing the interior design of wall paintings, decoration items, cut glass pots, prayer room or exchanging the utility of rooms
- Altering bed and bedroom arrangements

Part V: Vastu Tips for Room Position and Furniture Layout for Business and Industry

- The receptionist must face the entrance door or waiting lobby
- The cashier / accountant's room must be on the Northern side of the building and should sit facing towards the North.
- The room for sales promotion staff should be located in the Eastern corner of the building and they should sit facing the East
- Service and maintenance staff should be in the Southern corner of the building
- Chairman / MD's room should be on the South-West corner of the building and the seating should be facing towards the East

- R and D department should be located in the North-West corner
- The pantry / kitchen should be in the South-East corner
- Conference Room and new development planning should be located on the Eastern side of the building
- Pleasing and harmonious sounds are also good attractions, are lucky and encourage wealth building. Anything that creates good, soothing and inviting sounds like waterfalls, fountains, good music, musical chimes, musical clocks, natural sound of the breeze, etc. are considered as good
- Positioning and facing the desk, office table, work table, dining table, display table etc. has to be carefully oriented according to the environment and flow of energies
- Positioning and opening of doors as well as the number and size of windows has to be planned according to the orientation of the building and weather conditions
- Hanging beams in the rooms and corridors are wrong and must be avoided
- Vastu also says that exposed beams can cause an oppressive weight above us. If the beams are directly above our heads, they may cause heaviness, depression or headaches. If they are above our stomach while sleeping, they may cause indigestion problems
- Extra large beams over windows in the form of lintels can block the positive energy flowing into the house
- The study table or work table should never be placed below a hanging RCC beam or lintel
- No one should sit under a staircase
- A good-sized sun protection shade should be provided on the South and West sides, above the windows and doors
- A good number of doors or large windows should be provided on the North and North-Eastern side of the building
- The North or East walls of the building should never be blocked

Vastu for Modern Living

The most modern building whether it is a house or multi-storeyed commercial building, hospital, hotel restaurant, business establishment and small or big industries. People have again started believing in Vastu Shastra and even in other parts of the world they like incorporating the principles of the Vastu in their design. The Chinese are also firm believers of Vastu principles called Feng-Shui. It is an extremely ancient and well-developed system as far back as approximately 5000 years ago. Now in Hong-Kong, Singapore, Taiwan etc. the most modern buildings are designed and decorated adopting this ancient system.

One must possess sufficient knowledge of Vastu Vigyan (Science) and its application before advising or designing one's place of residence or work.

Part VI: General Tips on Interiors of Commercial Buildings, Houses and Flats

A few tips for interiors of houses, flats or commercial buildings:

1. In the living room, furniture, sofa sets etc. should be placed more towards the West and Southern side. The owners of the house should sit facing the East or North and the guest should occupy sofas facing West or South
2. Cash-Boxes (Treasury) or jewellery should be in the room towards the North, but if the box is heavy, it should be kept in the South, West or South-West corner. The person opening the locker should face the North
3. All heavy household items should be on the South and South-Western sides of the room.
4. All mirrors should be fixed on the North or East walls and not on the South and West walls. Consequently, the washbasins in the toilet too will have to be fixed on the North and East walls. Slope of the floor shall be towards the North-East

5. In the kitchen, grinders, fridge, shelf and other heavy items should be towards the South and West Walls. Even in the storeroom, racks should be on the S-West walls
6. In the dining room, while eating breakfast/lunch one should sit facing the East and while eating dinner one should sit facing the West
7. Television or computer set should be placed in the South/East corner of the living or drawing room or in the office
8. Bed or cot should be placed such that when one sleeps, the head must be directed towards the South, East or West. But never towards the North
9. Solar heaters should be fixed in the South East corner of the terrace. Overhead water tank should be in the South West corner of the terrace
10. Underground water tank should be in the North-East corner of the plot
11. Staircase and lift room should be located in the South, West or South-West corner
12. Stone sculptures, dry rock garden, mountain and landscaping should be in the South-West corner
13. Water bodies like well, bore-well, under ground storage tank, pump etc. should be in the North-Eastern zone of the plot
14. Water bodies should not be in front of any entrance door to the house
15. Entrance doors of two different houses should never be exactly opposite to each other

The Nectar of Life
(Water Therapy)

Water is the fountain of life and constitutes about 70 % of the total body weight. Water serves as a transport system for the nutrients we get from food. Water is required for inner cleanliness because it removes toxic wastes produced by the cells. Water keeps the body temperature stable.

Appetisers like salt, hot peppers, spices, limejuice and a heavy meal, increase the sensation of thirst. One should drink at least 9 glasses of water (2 litres) daily in addition to the water we get from fruits, vegetables and other foods. It is true that drinking water is good but excessive drinking can disturb the internal environment and may put an unnecessary burden on the kidneys, especially in patients suffering from kidney problems.

Water should be taken half an hour before the beginning of meal and half an hour after the meal. Drinking water during the meals dilutes the digestive juices and delays digestion. It also unnecessarily increases the bulk of the stomach contents, which is one of the potent causes of indigestion. If one still feels like drinking water during the meal, it should be taken in medicinal amounts. Drink water only when the food has left the stomach and it has emptied out. Liquid food should be kept in the mouth for as long as one can for proper mixing with the saliva.

Water must be sipped slowly. Keep every sip of water for a few seconds in the mouth to let it warm before it goes down the throat. Water taken in this manner quenches the thirst and gives enjoyment and greater satisfaction.

Longevity and Healthy Life Through Water Therapy

To experience the miracle of water therapy, water should be looked upon as a medicine. Drinking ample amounts of water can get rid of many diseases and is a simple cure for many ailments.

The Atharvaveda 7 and 57 are full of references to diseases that are curable through the various uses of water and vaporization. Atharvaveda 57.3 says: "Let it be health and joy to us. Let water be the universal medicine".

Water therapy declares the efficiency of water in so many words: water is beneficial, water is essence, water contains nectar, water is medicinal, water contains all medicinal properties.

Atharvaveda XIX, 2,8 is full of references to the healing power of water. Thus, it can be seen that water is a medicine finds ample references in our ancient lasp.

With the advent of modern medicines, human beings have forgotten this pure and simple but important therapy.

Consuming pure drinking water by the right method purifies the human body. It renders the colon more effective in forming new fresh blood, known in medical terms as "Haemotoplases". It is an undisputed fact that the mucous folds of the colon and intestines are activated by this method. The theory that new fresh blood is produced by the absorption of the nutrients of the food by the function of mucosal.

If the colon is cleaned, the nutrients of the food taken several times during the day will be absorbed and by the action of the mucous folds, they are turned into fresh blood. This blood is all-important in curing ailments and restoring health. Water should, therefore, be consumed in a regular pattern. Drinking ample amounts of water gives you a glowing skin and may protect you from diseases.

The best of all, it improves complexion and one would never have wrinkles even in the old age as the human body contains about 70% or more of water.

If one is already in good health, the use of Water Therapy upgrades one to perfect health so that life can be enjoyed to the fullest.

METHOD FOR USING WATER THERAPY

Step-I   Every night, before going to sleep, wash your face and brush your teeth properly. Do not eat or drink stimulating beverages or soft drinks after dinner.

Step-II Keep 1.25 kg. (1260 cc) of water in a clean copper pot by your bed side on a wooden stool (not on the floor or steel table).

Step-III After getting up in the morning, before washing your face, teeth, mouth, or even eyes, drink this water in one go (this is very important). The night saliva, which contains medicinal properties, has to be swallowed back into the body. Do not eat anything or have any beverages for the next 45 minutes. The water should be consumed preferably while sitting on the bed without putting the feet down on the floor or wear rubber slippers while consuming the water.

Initially small quantities of water which are acceptable to the body may be taken and the quantity of water be gradually increased to 1.25 litres at a stretch. However, more water can be consumed if it is acceptable to your body, as water in excess of the body's requirement will automatically go out. During the whole day, 4 to 5 litres of water should be consumed (not necessarily from the copper pot).

Water should not be taken half an hour before the meal, during the meal and one hour after the meal. Any drugs/medicines which are being taken may be reduced only in consultation with your physician after the improvement is felt in the physical condition.

Water Therapy is only a natural remedy that cleans the inner system of the body and helps in recovering faster. During the initial 2 to 3 weeks of commencement of this therapy, one may urinate excessively for about 3 to 4 times within the first few hours of drinking the water. However, the body system will accept this gradually and it will become a normal routine.

The diseases that can be cured by Water Therapy are Cancer, Diabetes, Tuberculosis, Arthritis, Constipation, Headache, Hypertension, Anemia, Rheumatism, Obesity, Sinusitis, Cough, Asthma, Tachycardia, Bronchitis, Meningitis, Urogenital diseases, Hyperacidity, Ophthalmic problems, Haemorrage, Opthalmia, Irregular Menstruation, Leuchorrea, Uterine Cancer, Cancer Of the Mammary Glands And Obesity.

Persons suffering from Arthritis and Rheumatism should practice water therapy twice a day for one week and thereafter once a day.

Our body needs water for breathing also, as our lungs must be moist to take in oxygen and excrete carbon dioxide. It is possible to lose half a litres of liquid each day by just exhaling. Hence, if sufficient quantities of water are not consumed, it can impair every aspect of the physiology.

In the words of Dr. Howard Flaks, a Bariatric (obesity) specialist in California, "By not drinking enough water, many people incur excess body fat, poor muscle tone and size, decreased digestive efficiency and organ function, increased toxicity in the body, joints, muscle soreness and water retention".

WHAT IS WATER RETENTION?

If we do not drink enough water, the body may retain water to compensate for the lack of sufficient supply. Paradoxically, drinking more water, not less, can sometimes eliminate fluid retention.

"Proper water intake is a key to weight loss," say obesity specialists.

"If people who are trying to lose weight do not drink enough water, the body metabolise the fat adequately. Retaining fluid also keeps the weight up."

The minimum quantity of water for a healthy person is 10 to 12 glasses a day or more if the person exercises regularly or lives in a hot climate.

–17–

Adopting the Vedic Culture

VEDIC SYSTEM FOR COPING WITH STRESS AND CHALLENGES

Most of us work hard for our children and would do anything for them. However, during the developmental period, between the ages of 5 to 12 years, a child struggles hard to gain personal independence and to deal with new feelings and emotions.

Factors like disruption in the family structure, lack of parental love and support and adverse effects of movies and television can further add to such struggles and may lead to anxiety, fear, sense of insecurity, depression and other psychosomatic stress disorders. It is now well established that these disorders are caused initially by disturbed conditions of the mind followed by derangements in one or more vital organs of the body.

The school is the most suitable place where the members of society can introduce an early educational programme, which can help the children to control their minds. At the same time, parental duties and responsibilities are equally important to give their children an upbringing in family traditions (Good Sanskars) and inject the Vedic Culture into their daily life at an early age.

One must breathe properly to ensure a maximum intake of oxygen for optimal growth and functioning of the body. As a part of ordinary breathing, many pollutants, including cigarette smoke are inhaled. In addition, blind use of stimulants, sedatives, drugs or other such substances of abuse also increases the formation of various encumbrances.

The body regards these as stressors or irritating stimuli that produce mucus. Mucus, along with other encumbrances gets deposited throughout the epithelial lining and other parts of the respiratory tract. Such depositions of encumbrances make the lungs rigid and inelastic. This reduces the total breathing capacity of the lungs, reduces breathing capacity and decreases the intake of oxygen per breath. This means less oxygen reaches the lungs.

We observe in our daily life that the pattern and rate of breathing are ordinarily irregular. For example, rapid and shallow during fear and anxiety; shallow inhalation and panting during anger, spasmodic and superficial during bereavement and sorrow, and, a feeling of suffocation during guilt.

Pranayama teaches us how to improve the flow of prana (life force) in the body and make breathing regular, comfortable, smooth and easy during stressful situations.

The human body continuously experiences stress that results in tension and too much uptightness in our lives. In a living state of our life, there are two planes in which the body functions; such as, seeing a picture, listening to music, touching the nose, eating sweets or smelling the scent.

In contrast, the beating of the heart, digestion of food, or absorption of oxygen from the lungs occur unconsciously without our knowledge or conscious use of our five senses.

Yogic Rishis and Munis have claimed that even those functions that take place unconsciously can be brought under conscious control.

Memories, anticipations, desires, fears, bad dreams and emotional pressures embedded in our subconscious mind disturb the order and peace of our conscious mind. To bring peace, one must learn how to control the mind.

Although use of tranquilizer drugs may help in bringing calmness of mind temporarily, these cannot change the environment because the disturbing stimuli are still present. The practice of yoga is one of the best alternatives since it targets the sense organs first in order to control the mind.

Healthy living depends mainly on the selection of food in addition to dwelling company and environment. A vast majority of our population is poor and does not get enough to eat and suffers from under nourishment. In contrast, over eating is common among the well to do.

Many of us are still obese, irrespective of being rich or poor. This is simply because we eat the wrong kind of food. The markets are flooded with all sorts of junk food, canned food, refined foods and synthetic beverages that have very little or no nutritional value. The younger generation is getting more and more addicted to such harmful foods due to very attractive advertisements and, also probably due to non-availability of home cooked food. Furthermore, we eat food in the wrong combinations, at the wrong time and in the wrong manner.

One should eat for the sake of health and efficiency and for the maintenance of the body, and not for the pleasure of eating or taste. Unhygienic eating is not conducive to the health of the mind and body. For a high level of health, one should eat just as much as would not cause a feeling of heaviness after a lapse of at least two hours.

In the human body, there are two processes - digestion, which provides nutrition and excretion, the process that purifies the body's environment by expelling all waste products from the body. Both these processes should work in harmony. Continuous overburdening of these processes will exhaust the energy resources of the body and may lead to poor health.

For physical and mental well-being, we must know what to eat, how much to eat, when to eat and how to eat.

If we carefully study the free animals and birds in the jungle; they never become sick, because they follow the principle of what to eat, how much to eat and when to eat.

Let us discuss this principle.

WHAT TO EAT?

Ancient people in their natural state sustained only on fruits and vegetables. These are positive foods and induce a high degree of purity in both body and mind. Positive foods are bulky, having a high fibre content and moisture. These foods are lighter and easy to digest.

On the other hand, negative foods are constipating because these have a high content of protein, starch and fat. An excessive intake of starch undergoes fermentation and produces carbon dioxide that is acidic. Hyper acidity causes palpitation, which is often mistaken for heart trouble. An excessive intake of proteins causes headache, fatigue, pain and swelling of the joints. Excess of fats causes difficulty in digestion of other foods and leads to coronary heart disease.

Various grains, fruits, vegetables and nuts are positive foods for humans. When well chewed and mixed with saliva, these foods are always easily assimilated. Studies have now shown that people who eat fresh fruit daily are healthier and are less prone to strokes and heart attacks.

Fresh fruits protect the body against cancer and obesity too. All canned foods and juices are negative foods because they contain preservatives and are not fresh. Tea, cocoa and coffee are depressants and unlock our own reserves that are consumed quickly.

Sweets should be taken sparingly because sugar is called "a Vitamin Thief." Fresh milk is believed to be a complete food but it produces mucus and can give rise to catarrhal diseases, which include, sinusitis, cough, bronchitis and pneumonia. Homemade yoghurt without any flavour is good for digestion.

How much to eat?

It is always healthy to eat a bit less than your capacity to digest, without bothering much about the calorie theory. One should never eat more than what the vital power can cope with. It has been shown by studies on monkeys that underfed animals had as twice as high as the levels of high density lipoprotein–the good cholesterol than the normal eating animals. The theory is that lowering calorie intake resets the body's metabolism for it to operate more efficiently. It is also hypothesized that perhaps people may live longer and better if they stop eating before they feel full. Overeating will make the food stay for a longer time than normal in the digestive canal.

Since food is a perishable commodity, it will deteriorate; starches will ferment, proteins will putrefy and foul smelling gases will be generated. Eating more than necessary can also increase the weight. For example, taking 3000 calories in excess of what is required in a week will increase your body weight by one kilogram a week. Eating one principal meal in a day is ideal. Eating twice a day is medium and eating thrice a day is bad. For a high level of health, only the minimum should be eaten. The body will be fit even without much exercise. The mind will be clear and calm and can concentrate more.

WHEN TO EAT?

One should only eat when keen natural hunger is present. True hunger arises only when the physical body is well rested and the mind is calm. If fatigue occurs, one must rest until hunger gets matured. During the interval, a cold bath and prayers also help.

According to the Vedic principles, " when the stools and urine have been expelled, the mind is clean and the sense of humour is functioning normally. When a clean wind is felt, when the digestive energy is at its height; the whole body is light, the senses are clear and efficient". Only then one should eat the food ordained by hygiene. Hunger should not be killed immediately after it is born. It should be allowed to mature.

HOW TO EAT?

One spends all the time available in earning one's bread but does not devote enough time to enjoying that hard-earned bread. Sometimes a principal meal is finished in five minutes. Those who do so, forget that they do not have teeth in their stomach. One should always eat slowly.

Experts say that eating slowly prevents overeating. It takes at least fifteen minutes for the brain to signal fullness. Therefore, take about thirty minutes to consume a principal meal for fullest enjoyment and better health. If you are worried and angry or scared, it is always good to walk around or chat with your friends or wait for sometime before eating.

Wash your face and hands before eating. It is not only hygienic but it also stimulates the secretion of saliva.

If possible, eat while sitting with folded (crossed) legs. This allows uniform entry of food into the stomach. Sit in a comfortable asana, with a pleasant and clean surrounding environment.

Talk less, do not watch T.V. or read the newspaper during a meal. The mind will be diverted and may suppress the process of digestion if the concentration is elsewhere.

Do not mix too many different types of food in one meal. If there is no choice, taste each item separately at the beginning of the meal. This will stimulate the secretion of different enzymes, which help in digestion of various kinds of foods in a meal.

Chew the food well so that digestion of starch can proceed properly in the mouth.

Do not do any heavy work just after eating. One must lie down on the left side for 10 minutes after lunch. After dinner, take a walk in the open air for 10 to 15 minutes. This will help in improving the digestion.

Drink water one hour before eating or one hour after eating. Drinking water along with the food or during the meal can suppress the formation of saliva.

–18–
The Magical Gifts of Yoga and Meditation

OBJECTIVE

To provide readers with the basic but essential knowledge of yoga, especially on the practice of Yogasana as one of the means to promote physical health and mental concentration in order to deal effectively with the stress of Modern Life and observe cleanliness of body, mind soul and environment.

The word Yoga is derived from the Sanskrit word 'Yuj'.

Yoga, therefore, is defined as a method of training designed to unite the body to the soul, and the individual soul to the universal soul. It develops moral character, makes children more caring and loving towards their parents, teachers and friends. Yoga is for everybody. Yoga is good for persons of all ages.

Yogic concepts and techniques, which remained scattered in the Vedic Literature, were collected and put together as "Yoga Sutra" by Patanjali. The Yoga Sutras do not set forth any religious dogma but indicate how liberation can be attained by disciplined activity.

In fact, practice of Yoga cultivates emotional stability by:

(1) Bringing involuntary muscles under the control of the mind
(2) Liberating the mind from its sensory organs
(3) Destroying the "mind" for the liberation of "soul"

Yoga is a method by which one can attain perfection in life by realising one's divine potential and then to make an all out attempt to unite with it.

Types of Yoga

The main goal of practicing yoga is to harmonise the body, mind and spirit so that they function with complete unison amongst themselves. This goal can be achieved by following either a single type or by combining various types of Yoga. Each of these types has been tailor-made for different kinds of persons. However, all these types begin with the same moral preliminaries. The difference between exercise and Yoga is that in exercise, the person gets tired and exhausted, while in Yoga, the person's muscles get relaxed and he feels refreshed.

The different types of Yoga are:

1. Gyaan Yoga

It is a way to understand Yoga through knowledge and is intended for spiritual aspirants who are capable of thinking and reasoning. A philosophical mind responds quickly to this type of Yoga. The aim of this Yoga is to teach how to 'know' with the soul, rather than how to 'think' with the mind. Since the mind thinks and gives knowledge, and the soul knows and gives wisdom.

2. Bhakti Yoga

It is a way of Yoga through love. It is suitable for those who are devotional or loving type and have a great capacity for feeling. It teaches up to an extent where one no longer finds faults with the world or with any body.

3. Karma Yoga

It is a way through work and suits those who are active and the working type. This type of Yoga teaches how to perform the right action at the right time and renounce the fruits of their action.

4. Raja Yoga

It is the way through psychological exercises. It is designed for persons who basically have a scientific bent of mind. They respond more to mental stimuli rather than to sense stimuli. It combines Dharna (concentration) and Dhyana (meditation) to control the mind and strengthen the power of concentration.

5. Hatha Yoga

The essence of Hatha Yoga is to balance and equalise the practice that combines Asana (posture), Pranayama (breath control), Mudra (hand gestures) and Nadaanusandhana (cleansing processes) in order to preserve the physical life to the highest perfection without influencing much of our mental and spiritual life.

6. Kundalini Yoga

According to Tantric Literature, there is a chain of seven or centres in the body, the lowest in the sacral region and the highest at the center of the brain. From the modern physiological point of view, these can be equated with various autonomic ganglia. Normally, Kundalini Shakti remains dormant at the lowest Chakra as a potential energy. Seated habits organised around fear and insecurity keep this energy suppressed so that it cannot gather enough force to move up. By constant practice, one awakens this latent power and is able to ascend it though the chain of Chakras at will. Thus, one can control the autonomic and sensory inputs that enable one to increase the power of the mind.

THE CHAKRAS

- *Muladhara Chakra (Sacral plexus)* is situated at the root of the spinal cord between the genital organs and the anus. This is the place where the Kundalini Shakti remains in a dormant state. It regulates the functions of the sex glands and kidneys.
- *Svadhisthana Chakra (Lumbar Plexus)* is situated four inches below the navel and regulates functions of the colon and rectum.
- *Manipura Chakra (Caeliac Plexus)* is situated at the level of the navel and regulates the functions of the adrenal glands, stomach and intestines.

- *Anahata Chakra (Cardiac Plexus)* is situated at the level of the heart and regulates the functions of heart and thymus gland.
- *Vishuddha Chakra (Pulmonary Plexus)* is situated in the throat below the larynx and regulates the functions of the thyroid glands and lungs.
- *Ajna Chakra (Cervical Plexus)* is situated between the eye brows (the third eye) and regulates the functions of the pituitary gland.
- *Sahastrar Chakra (Choroid Plexus)* is situated at the crown (Center of the brain) and regulates the functions of autonomic and central nervous systems. It is the center of awareness.

7. Ashtanga Yoga

As mentioned above, there are several types of yoga, some mainly dealing with the mental and spiritual health or specific problems in the body. Patanjali has described one of the best types of integrated approach. It consists of eight limbs and is therefore called as Ashtanga Yoga.

(I) Yama (Abstentions)

One can practice abstention through Ahimsa, by not causing any bodily or mental injury by our deeds or words.

(II) Niyama (Observances)

It involves the practice of:
  (a) *Saucha*, cleanliness of both body and mind
  (b) *Santosha*, contentment of the mind
  (c) *Tapas*, involves a constant practice of self-discipline and austerity
  (d) *Svadhyaya*, self study of sacred books
  (e) *Pranidhana*, dedicate all our actions and fruits of our actions to God.

(III) Asana

A posture that makes the body comfortable. Through the practice of asanas, one not only gets steadiness in bodily health but also attains tranquility of mind.

- *Pranayama*

The practice of regular inhalation and exhalation of breath. It is conducive to the calmness of the body and mind.

- *Pratyahara*

It is the gathering up of the sensory organs from external objects and turning them inward to the object of meditation. This helps in controlling the mind and thus restrains the sensory organs.

- *Dharna*

It is concentrating the mind on a particular point. The object may be external or internal. It increases the power of concentration and is the first step towards meditation.

- *Dhyana (Meditation)*

It is an unbroken flow of knowledge at that point. Dharna is usually intervened by contrary thoughts. Dharana turns into Dhyana when uninterrupted by contrary thoughts.

- *Samadhi*

In Dhyana there are three factors—the object of meditation, the act of meditation and the meditator. In Samadhi, all these factors merge into one.

Mantra

Mantra is a word composed of certain letters arranged in a definite sequence of sounds, for example, OM or AUM. Chanting of OM in Hindu Philosophy is necessary for carrying out Yoga. Chanting of this word involves the abdomen, throat, tongue, teeth and the lips. The sound of this word produces vibrations that gradually lead the mind out of its normal thinking process into

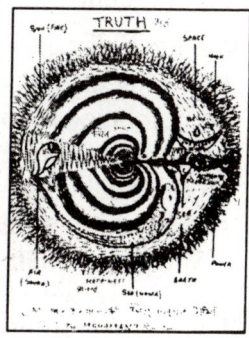

silence. Thus, silent repetition of OM during the practice of yoga does not allow distraction of the mind by internal or external sources.

Mudra

Mudra is a gesture made with the hands or fingers during prayer or yoga practice. Our body is made up of five gross elements. Each finger of our hand represents one of these elements. For example, the thumb represents fire; the index finger, air; the middle finger, space, the ring or third finger, earth and the little finger, water.

Touching the fingers in various combinations helps to remove the deficiency or the excess of these elements in the body. Touching the tip of the first finger lightly with the tip of the thumb of the same hand during Yoga increases the flow of energy towards the brain and improves the thinking power and memory.

Yoga Mudras

The five Yoga Mudras are:

The fingers of our hand also represent the five elements, and they act accordingly.

(1) The Thumb represents FIRE (Agni)
(2) The Index Finger represents AIR (Vayu)
(3) The Middle Finger represents SPACE (Shunya)
(4) The Ring Finger represents EARTH (Prithvi)
(5) The Little Finger represents WATER (Jal)

We have discussed and studied in Vastu that when all the five elements are in proper balance in our building design, are in relation to the climatology of the country and blended with the weather conditions, we can safely assume that the house or building is healthy and the occupants of the building experience good health, wealth and peace.

Similarly, when these five elements are properly balanced in our body, we experience good health and balance of mind.

However, if there is an imbalance of the elements, one

suffers corresponding ailments. To cure and balance, one can practice the following mudras:
1. *Varun Mudra:* Join the tips of the little finger and the thumb together. This helps in curing skin disease and brings luster to dry skin and makes it smooth.
2. *Prithvi Mudra:* Join the tips of the ring finger and the thumb together. This helps in curing weakness of mind and body. Gives positive energy and injects life force into the body.
3. *Gyan-Dhyan Mudra:* Join the tips of the index finger and the thumb together. This helps in reducing loss of memory, sleeplessness and lack of concentration.
4. *Surya Mudra:* Place the ring finger at the base of the thumb and press gently. This helps in reducing the excess cholesterol in the blood.
5. *Hridaya Mudra:* Keep the index finger between the point at the base of the thumb and keep the tips of both middle and ring fingers on the tip of thumb. This helps in curing asthma and breathing problems. It also helps the palpitation of the heart.
6. *Amit Mudra:* Fold the three fingers of the left hand and cover half the nails of the three fingers with the thumb. The little finger remains extended. Rest the left palm on the left knee. The fingers of the right hand should be open, just rest it on the right knee, palm facing down. Close the eyes. This makes your mind stress free.

The Yoga Mudras explained above are easy to practise. To get effective results, one must practise the Mudras twice a day for 20 to 30 minutes at a stretch.

Touching the fingers in various combinations helps to remove the deficiency or the excess of these elements in the body. Touching the tip of the first finger lightly with the tip of the thumb of the same hand increases the flow of energy towards the brain and improves the thinking power and memory.

Concept of Asana

The word Asana comes from the Sanskrit root "As", "to sit", meaning a sitting or meditative posture. It is an elastic attitude of the body and mind suitable for physical, mental and spiritual health. Asana is the third limb of Ashtanga Yoga that prepares an individual towards meditation. Yogis developed various asanas thousands of years ago, by watching wild animals, how they moved, how they rested and how they cured themselves when sick. Therefore, many of the asanas took the names of animals, reptiles and birds, which include lion hare, fish, cobra, peacock and tortoise.

Practice of Asanas

Postural distortion goes hand in hand with muscular-physiological imbalances. Distortion and muscular imbalances may result from trauma, disease, work and sport or from chronic emotional states such as depression or fear. While other forms of therapy may address these causative factors, Yogasanas associated with the techniques of breathing and relaxation are powerful tools for not only correcting postural distortions but also for maintaining proper concentration of various hormones in the blood. Asanas strengthen all the Chakras and, in turn, restore natural balance and health of body and mind.

Yoga *versus* Physical Exercise

Scientific investigations have shown that the practice of yogasanas has a definite advantage over the regular muscular exercises which athletes practice every day in sports.

Most of the ordinary muscular exercises are repetitive and involve the utilisation of a lot of energy, whereas in yoga practice, a particular posture is maintained continuously for a definite period in order to concentrate the bodily and mental powers without using much of his muscular energy.

Ordinary muscular exercises improve blood circulation only of voluntary muscles whereas yoga exercises are directed towards improvement in the circulation of all the vital organs.

Yoga exercises, if done systematically under proper guidance, are not painful and are very relaxing.

Types of Asanas

There are more than 1000 asanas; out of which only a few have been placed under two broad categories. A right combination of two types of asanas, relaxes muscle, restores energy and improves both physical and mental health by exercising and massaging all the internal organs.

Some of the important asanas are described below:

(1) Dhyanasana:
These postures are employed during meditation. The main aim of practicing this posture is to control the mind and increase the power of concentration.

(2) Siddhasana:
It is placing one heel firmly against the premium and fixing the other foot above the penis. It is used for pranayama, ordinary worship and prayer. It is not prescribed for women. Its benefit includes balance and patience of mind.

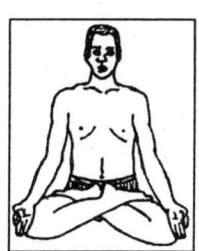

(3) Padmasana (Lotus Pose):
It is placing the right foot on the left thigh and the left foot on the right thigh and the hands clasped together in the lap with the palms facing up. It is also used for pranayama, meditation and prayer. It tones up all the nerves and the tendons in the legs; cures gout in the ankles and toes; relieves constipation, indigestion and wind.

(4) Yogasana (Yoga Pose):
This is similar to Padmasana and is one of the most popular sitting postures adopted to practice pranayama and meditation to control the mind. It puts all the nerves and parts of the legs in proper order. It cures lung diseases and also has a soothing effect on the mind.
People who practice this posture with faith learn how to control their negative thoughts and emotions and thus will be able to concentrate better in studies or doing their jobs.

(5) Svastikasana (Svastika Pose): is placing the left foot against the right thigh and the right foot against the left thigh. Keep the body erect and arms stretched so that the hands project beyond the knees. This asana helps those whose feet remain unusually hot or cold or sweat too much.

(6) Vajrasana (Adamantine Pose):
Involves sitting on the heels with the spine erect. It makes the body hard like a diamond; helps digestion and reduces lethargy and sloth.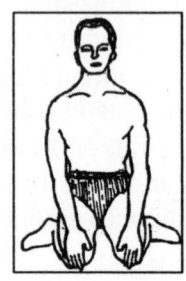

(7) Shavasana (Corpse Pose)
is lying supine on the ground like a corpse. It wards off fatigue, mental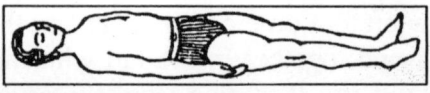
tension and feeling of tiredness; relaxes the body and mind, cures asthama, obesity and high blood pressure.

(8) Bhujanagasana (Cobra Pose):
is lying down on the abdomen, supporting the weight on the palms, raising the chest and head thrown backward. It gives flexibility to the spine; improves functions of the abdominal

organs and removes constipation; helps prevent and cure eye diseases; checks nose bleeding; it is good for women having menstrual problems.

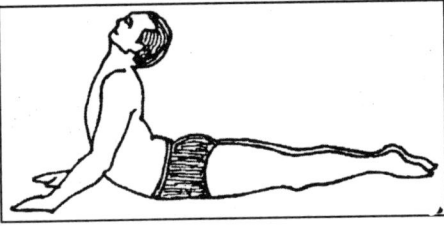

(9) Halaasana (Plough Pose): is lying back, slowly carrying both the legs towards the head and stretching them as far as possible. It strengthens the glands in the neck and stomach; exercises the spine; reduces fat around the abdomen and waist. This asana is also a good cure for menstrual problems.

(10) Dhanurasana (Bow pose):

is lying prone with hands directing over the back. Bend the legs at knees and hold the ankles firmly and raise the trunk as far as possible. It keeps the spine free from aches and pains; expands the chest; cures obesity and makes one slim and smart. It increases appetite and cures indigestion.

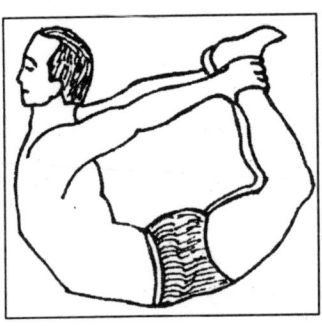

(11) Bhastrikasana (Bellow Pose): is lying on the back and bringing both the thighs in contact with the chest in a flexed condition. Catch both the legs firmly with both the hands. It removes abdominal gas, cures

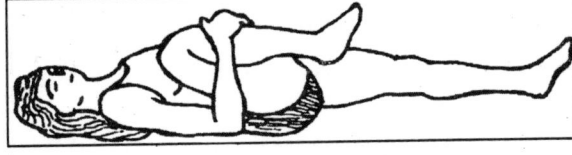

indigestion, removes excess stomach fat, and cures headache and high blood pressure.

(12) Matsyendrasana (Twist Pose):

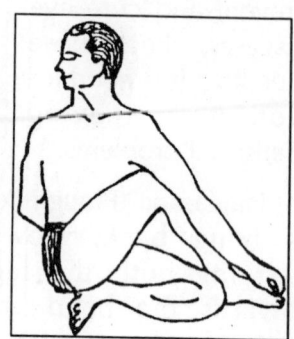

is placing the right foot at the root of the left thigh. Encircle the right knee with the left leg, hold the two feet with the opposite hands, twist the body and stay. It removes excessive calcium accumulation in the spine; stimulates gastric fire and thus help cure diseases including diabetes mellitus.

(13) Paschimottanasana (Head to Knee Pose):

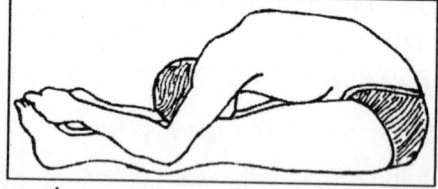

is stretching both the legs straight on the ground, holding the big toes with respective hands and placing the forehead on the knees. It stretches the muscles of the spine; removes excess abdominal fat, constipation and chest defects; helps patients of diabetes and cures eye diseases.

(14) Virasasana (Brave Pose):

is sitting on the toes with both the heels under the buttocks and hands placed on thighs. It is helpful for strengthening joints of the feet and fingers and tones up abdominal viscera; cures hernia and urinary diseases.

Technique for Yogasana

The following steps must be followed while doing yogasanas:

(I) Body Positioning

- Sit on a clean insulated asana (mat) placed on a dry

floor. Cross your legs in such a way that each foot rests with its sole facing up on the opposite thigh. Make sure that both the heels either meet or are as close to each other as possible under the navel.
- Stretch both the hands out, palms up, over each knee. Touch the tip of the first finger lightly with the tip of the thumb of the same hand keeping the other three fingers straight.
- Keep your spinal cord (back bone) and neck right up to the base of the skull fully erect and straight.

(II) Concentration

Fix your eyes (it is best to leave the eyes half open) on a point somewhere between the eye brows or on the tip of the nose.

(III) Chant the mantra, OM silently and rhythmically throughout the period. Breathe normally through both nostrils. Do not hold the breath.

(IV) One may then choose the suitable Dhyanasanas. Once each step is perfected, it is easy to practice the entire procedure. Initially, one can practice this posture as long as one feels comfortable and relaxed and can keep on increasing the duration with practice.

Benefits of Yoga and Meditation

1. Improved concentration of mind
2. Increased memory and thinking power
3. Reduced anxiety and fear of examination, test or interview
4. Increase energy and strength in the body
5. Increase tolerance to stress
6. Balance the breathing rhythm
7. Increase ability of blood to absorb and carry oxygen
8. Increase storage of oxygen

The Practice of Yogasanas

- Strengthens the spine and relieves compression of the nerves

- Increases the power of thinking and improves the memory
- Increases concentration in studies
- Reduces anxiety and fear of examination
- Clears the lungs and improves breathing
- Increases blood and lymph circulation
- Develops moral conduct and creativity
- Prepares children to be more loving and caring towards each other
- Enables children to respect their parents, teachers and friends
- Brings peace in the home, school and community
- Restores energy and makes the body healthy
- Increases the biological age

Yogasana should preferably be performed
- Under the instruction of experienced teachers
- Slowly and smoothly, avoiding strains and jerks during all the steps
- In the morning and evening when the stomach is empty
- In a clean and open environment e.g. garden or in a room near the window
- Using minimum and loose clothing of cotton
- Bare footed
- Without talking
- With full faith and devotion

Conclusion

If we have to equip ourselves to meet the challenges of the future, we must examine the forces that are now transforming our modern activity and living style of people. The most talked about topic these days is how to base the building activity on the principles of Vastu Shastra, the science of planning and construction formulated by our ancestors some 5000 years ago, giving the principles of planning and orientation for the building activities, related to safety and hygiene. It shows good results when understood and followed properly. It is user oriented and makes everyone's life peaceful, prosperous and happier.

Living in harmony with Nature is the Art of Living. If the foundation is not correct, good results can never be achieved. Vedas are our heritage. And heritage is like roots to trees. We, therefore, have to go back to our roots and study the most elementary and important principles of Vedic Knowledge for a healthier and prosperous life. The goal of the discourses is to successfully harness the resources of our rich heritage and give strength to the individual and thereby to the community as a whole.

A theory that claims to be scientific cannot claim to be final. Theories that exist have to be tested and modified, elaborated and refuted. For the reasons given previously, it is unlikely that practitioners will, of their own initiative, undertake the testing of any theory. A new field of practice research is emerging. Further development of methods requires collaboration between practitioners and researchers on case studies. There is no single method that can be used on all occasions. The appropriate methods for any given task are defined by the social nature of the task.

The Vedas play a colossal role, not only in forming a frame around existing activities, but also in ensuring that the frame may create new activities. Only by means of fully understanding the role of modern living to find solutions, for obtaining good result.

It is more important to raise the correct questions rather than to give correct answers to the wrong questions.

It is worthwhile to form a habit of saying "yes" to a new idea. The trouble with an average person is that he does not sufficiently trust himself to deliver ideas or to create new ideas.

After the Second World War, architectural practices raced fast towards modernisation adopting the bureaucratic values resulting in worldwide pollution, environmental and ecological problems, with no peace of mind under any kind of shelter, particularly under modern living.

Bridging the Two Cultures

Western culture is like a vast desert as compared to the unlimited ocean of Vedic knowledge. India is the source, the fountainhead of this vast ancient Vedic Science available on the planet today.

The word is out! It is now an open secret that this Vedic knowledge is the most complete and elevated instruction given to mankind. However, on the world scale this open secret is still relatively unknown.

When Vastu Science is presented through the most modern technological advances, this sublime information will be easily understood and be available to people in all walks of life.

This is the first major attempt in history to present this vast Vedic philosophy coupled with the latest high-tech, multi media systems of the west.

India must give this Vedic knowledge to the world. The 'Vedas' give a whole new look to the world of Vedic Architecture, Art and Science, scientifically, artistically and philosophically in practically every value of knowledge. There will be some shocking encounters to what is accurately known in this material world as Deductive Thought.

Conclusion

The East had a great vision in the way of its Vastu Shastras and Vedic understanding, but it is lacking materially. The West has abundant ' resources' and advanced technology but little spiritual vision. The harmony on this combination of East-West brings a perfect whole and a new revolution will evolve in the field of Modern Living.

Keeping this in mind, the author has founded a Charitable Trust **"Research Institute of Vedic Culture" (NGO)** in affiliation with Vastu Research Centre and World Academy of Spiritual Sciences (WASS) wherein an attempt has been made to educate and spread the Vedic Culture. In order to promote Vedic knowledge and give due recognition to the scholars who do the research work in occult sciences, the Trust is awarding degrees through research thesis in association with the Zoroastrian College (Mumbai).

To know more about our ancient Vedic Science and to go deeper into this subject, contact the Course Advisor at the following address:

Research Institute of Vedic Culture
W - 151, Greater Kailash, Part I
New Delhi - 110 048.
India
Phone: (011) 2924 2224,
E-mail:- vrcvastu@eth.net

BOOKS OF RELATED INTEREST FROM NAB

STHAPATYA VED-VASTU SASTRA
Ideal Homes, Colony and Town Planning
—*Niketan Anand Gaur*

Sthapatya Ved embraces the concept of the holistic origin of the universe. This concept envisages the view that all forms of creativity originate from transcendental consciousness. In this process it completely unites the mind and body, in the process of creativity. Sthapatya Ved is a branch of one of the principal Veds, the Atharva Ved.

ISBN: 978-81-7822-042-0

VASTU VIDYA
The Indian Art of Placement
—*Juliet Pegrum*

Vastu Vidya helps you design and organise your home or workplace to improve your good fortune and encourage wellbeing. Vastu Vidya (literally "dwelling science"-sometimes known simply as Vastu) seeks to align the places where we live and work with the energy of the cosmos and put us in harmony with our surroundings. Interest in Vastu is now re-emerging in India and growing rapidly in the West.

ISBN: 978-81-7822-047-5

VASTU SCIENCE FOR 21ST CENTURY
To enjoy the gift of nature
—*Prof. B.B. Puri*

"*Vastu Science for 21st Century*, is truly having its sense to enjoy the gift of nature. In this part of the world, it is very important to know the truth about the Vastu Shastra, and I found complete answer in this book. It is further interesting to know that in order for our lives to be truly peaceful, balanced and healthy, we must live in accordance with the law of nature, rather than against nature.

ISBN: 978-81-7822-107-6